UNIVERSALISM 101

God Is Love

AN INTRODUCTION FOR LEADERS OF
UNITARIAN UNIVERSALIST CONGREGATIONS

RICHARD TRUDEAU

Copyright © 2009 Richard Trudeau
All rights reserved.

ISBN: 1-4392-5143-6
ISBN-13: 9781439251430
Library of Congress Control Number: 2009907528
BookSurge Publishing

TABLE OF CONTENTS

A LETTER TO THE READER ·················· v
Supplement: You Become What You Eat

CHAPTER 1: I DISCOVER UNIVERSALISM·········· 1
Supplement: The Off-Center Cross • Shouldn't There Be Other Symbols Too? • "You Should Lose the Cross." • The UUA Logo

CHAPTER 2: UNIVERSALISM IN A NUTSHELL ···· 13
Supplement: God Is Love • God Is Love ? ! • Lincoln Recalls an Old Baptist

CHAPTER 3: UNIVERSALISM AND
UU RENEWAL ···················· 20
Supplement: The Elephant in the Room • Bringing Jesus Out the Door with Them (Dave Johnson) • Also Free to Keep • One Mountain, One Special Path • Humanists for Jesus • Other Things Universalism Has to Offer • Rev. Lovejoy on UUism (*The Simpsons*) • Universalism for Young People (Elizabeth Strong)

CHAPTER 4: "WHAT'S THE DIFFERENCE BETWEEN UNIVERSALISM AND UNITARIANISM?"················ 41
Supplement: The Winchester Profession • Misplacing Our History • The MLK-Universalist Connection • We Need *All* Our History

• Universalists Leading the Way: Child Dedications • Universalists Leading the Way: Children's Sunday • Universalists Leading the Way: Christmas (Stephen Nissenbaum) • Universalists Leading the Way: Antislavery • Universalists Leading the Way: Unitarianism! • Universalists Leading the Way: Women's Ordination • Universalist Decline • Snubbed • Theodore Parker on Universalism

CHAPTER 5: UNIVERSALIST CULTURE · · · · · · · · · 61
Some Leftovers Feed the Soul (William J. Hamilton III) • Universalist Chutzpah • Coffee Hour • The Ten Commandments Revisited (Patrick O'Neill) • Giving a Different Kind of Finger • Universalism and Class Diversity • Dead Over a Century but Evangelizing Still • The Dana Vespers • Carl Sandburg and the Spirit of Universalism • Who Are These "Universalists," and What Do They Want? • Church Sign

CHAPTER 6: UNIVERSALIST SPIRITUALITY · · · · · · 74
Supplement: Suggestion to Persons Entering Heaven (Mark Twain)

NOTES · 85

SUGGESTED READING · · · · · · · · · · · · · · · · · · 90

INDEX · 92

A Letter to the Reader

Few Unitarian Universalists (UUs), lay or ordained, know much about Universalist theology. On many occasions the *term* "Universalism" is used, but usually to refer to only one idea lifted from the network of ideas that historic Universalism comprised. For example, Universalism is often reduced to the idea that God is love, or that one should be open to insights from world religions, or that one should pay attention to the heart as well as the head. All such reductions are misleading.

On other occasions, Universalism is ignored altogether. It was completely off Paul Rasor's radar screen, for example, in his otherwise-admirable *Faith Without Certainty* (Boston: Skinner House, 2005).

A related problem is that few UUs know much about Universalist history or culture. This is relevant because Universalist theology was shaped by Universalist experience.

With the loss of Universalist perspective, our combined Unitarian Universalist religious movement is being impoverished. Universalism was different from Unitarianism. It originated among laypeople, not clergy. It drew on the experience of a less privileged social class. Its message was more radical, its scope was larger, and its taproot went deeper into the heart.

I have tried to present all of Universalism's distinctive ideas and make clear their relationships to each other. I have done so using a variety of approaches—essays, details from my own biography, anecdotes, laments, meditations, even jokes. I have also included some things by other writers.

If you are a Unitarian Universalist and, like many UUs, you call yourself simply "Unitarian," I hope you won't take offense if some of what I say about Unitarianism strikes you as uncomplimentary. I am not speaking of contemporary Unitarian Universalism (UUism) but rather the original American Unitarianism of the 1800s.

I also hope you won't take offense when I *am* speaking of contemporary UUism, but in critical terms. I don't think I say anything controversial—anything that was not, for example, in *Engaging Our Theological Diversity*, the 2005 report of the Unitarian Universalist Association's Commission on Appraisal. I have been involved with the UU movement—as an observer, then a friend, then a member, and now a minister—for almost fifty years. The UU movement is my spiritual home. I want to make it stronger.

I intend this book to be of service to the UU movement, so I want it to be *correct*. If you think I am in error on any point, please let me know. You may contact me by e-mail at Universalism101@gmail.com. Thank you.

Richard Trudeau

A Letter to the Reader

Supplement

You Become What You Eat

In 1960-61, when the Unitarian and Universalist denominations combined, the Universalists—less prosperous, less educated, less confident, and outnumbered five to one—were afraid of being swallowed up.

For a while it looked as if their fears were justified. Both Universalist seminaries were closed. The Universalist Service Committee was dissolved (and *Universalist* spliced into the name of the Unitarian Service Committee). And in town after town, once the Universalist church had gamely changed its name to "Unitarian Universalist" church, people started calling it "the Unitarian church." "There are no more Universalists," one man said. "We're all Unitarians now."

In a way he was right. *Unitarian Universalist* is a mouthful, and it's hard not to shorten it to *Unitarian* (though more and more of us are learning to say *UU* instead). But in another way, the reverse is true—we're all Universalists now. As the Rev. Dick Fewkes remarked, "You become what you eat."

Unitarianism was about freedom, reason, and tolerance. Universalism held those values too, but emphasized what it called "the supreme worth of every human personality." God loves everybody, Universalists said. God's love is universal.

This central Universalist sentiment has become the defining characteristic of our combined movement. Some of us may say we're "Unitarians," but we're Unitarian *Universalists*. You become what you eat.

Chapter 1: I Discover Universalism

I'm not a birthright Universalist or even a birthright UU. Universalism is something I stumbled on and fell in love with. And like all converts, I think what's been good for me would be good for many others.

I was raised in a mainstream Christian denomination—which shall be nameless—in which, I would say in retrospect, I was religiously violated; by which I mean that my natural religious curiosity was suffocated by the imposition of dogmas that were obsolete and terrifying. At seventeen, I left that church, and for the next fifteen years I did not attend any church and had nothing to do with organized religion. For fifteen years, my sanctuary was the woods, where I went to walk when I needed to think about something, or was sad, or frightened. For fifteen years, my fellow congregants were my friends, with whom I swapped shoptalk about life. And for fifteen years, my sermons were books that I read about the history of Christianity, the Bible, and world religions. Then, in my early thirties, I began to attend Unitarian Universalist churches, and I did so with a tremendous sense of relief and homecoming. And I fashioned a new UU faith for myself by drawing on bits and pieces from many sources. The principal source was humanism, but I also drew from Judaism, Taoism, Buddhism, and the study of nature.

After attending UU churches for several years, my circumstances changed, and I began attending a church that had a Universalist heritage. Theologically it was a mainstream

UU church, but the building contained artifacts that were evocative of the church's past. In particular, there was a large off-center cross on the front wall of the sanctuary. I couldn't take my eyes off it. I didn't like the cross in the circle, but I was fascinated by the fact that it was off to the side, and by the empty space at the center. At coffee hour that day, and on subsequent Sundays, I asked old-timers what the symbol meant. And based on what they told me, and also on my own imagination, I evolved an understanding of the symbol that turned out to be pretty close to what its designers intended it to convey.

The circle represents the universe. The empty space at the center represents the mystery at the heart of the universe that people call God. The cross represents Christianity—one path toward God and the path from which Universalism (and UUism) has grown; it is off to the side to leave room for other points of view and to acknowledge the validity of other paths toward God.

Week after week, month after month, I sat in my pew staring at that symbol, and I continued to feel uncomfortable at the sight of the cross within the circle. Eventually I started asking myself questions. "Richard, if your new UU faith is so inclusive, why does it include nothing from your Christian past? Richard, if you're so tolerant, why are you so intolerant of Christianity? Richard, why are you still so angry?" At last I saw that there was no choice but to embark on the difficult and exasperating task of trying to take my childhood religion apart. It took a lot of thinking and talking and studying, but after a few years, I felt I had actually accomplished this. And when my childhood religion lay before me disassembled, I noticed that it had lost the power to hurt me. I felt healed.

I felt as if I were standing before four piles. First, there was a big pile of toxic waste—hurtful things, poisonous things. Next was another large pile of things that were not hurtful, particularly, but that just seemed silly. And then there were two smaller piles. There was a pile of things that didn't seem silly—they still made good theological sense. Finally, there was a pile of things that didn't make much sense, but that *felt* good. And for the first time, I felt free to incorporate elements from those last two piles into my adult UU faith. These things had been inaccessible to me because they had been locked in combination with things that were hurtful or nonsensical. Now they were free, and I was able to reappropriate them. I treasure these things because they come from so far back in my personal past, and because of them my UU faith is now much more my own.

As a result of this experience, I have come to think that our congregations should be not so much "decontamination chambers" where people wash away their former religions, but rather workshops where they confront them.

In the course of taking my childhood religion apart, I was forced to make distinctions that I had never completely made. I'd like to mention three: one about the Bible, one about Jesus, and one about the cross.

The first distinction was between the religious right's view of the Bible and that of modern scholarship. To the religious right, it's a single book, with a single author, expressing a single point of view. To modern scholarship, it's a library of many books, by many different authors, expressing many different points of view.

I'm reminded of a joke I heard from the Rev. Patricia Bowen. A man dies and wakes up in heaven, and to his great surprise, learns that people worship in heaven as they had on earth. On an orientation tour, his guide shows him a stone church with stained-glass windows and incense wafting out, saying, "Those are the Episcopalians." He is shown a Shinto shrine, a synagogue, an ashram, a mosque, a Presbyterian church, and so on—you can spin this joke out as long as you like. Eventually they come to a clearing deep in the woods, where people are sitting in a circle, drinking coffee, and arguing. "Those are the Unitarian Universalists," the guide says. "They're arguing about whether they're here."

This is how I learned to think of the Bible. The Bible is like a bunch of UUs sitting around arguing. The various books are arguing with each other. The book of Job is arguing with the book of Leviticus. The book of P, one of the sources of Genesis, is arguing with another of the sources of Genesis, the book of J. The Bible is a discussion—it's not the word of God, but words about God.

The second distinction I had to make was between Jesus and Christ. This way of putting it can be confusing because a lot of people think of *Christ* as Jesus' last name. But *Christ* is a title mainstream Christianity uses for the being it claims is the son of God, who died for the sins of humanity, and was raised on the third day. I had to learn to distinguish Christ from Jesus, the person. Jesus seems to have been someone like Martin Luther King Jr.—an eloquent, courageous, religiously-motivated social reformer. I eventually came to understand him as a latter-day Israelite prophet—a critic of the status quo, a defender of the powerless, someone who was calling Israelite religion back to what he understood to be its first principles—someone whose eloquent restatements of ancient Israelite ethical principles still move people today, across all the centuries and despite all the intervening theological nonsense.

I finally had to make a distinction about the cross—between its Christian meaning and its historic meaning. The reason that mainstream Christianity is so enamored of the cross is that mainstream Christianity places great significance on Jesus' death. In the ancient creed, his career is reduced to a comma: "born of the virgin Mary, suffered under Pontius Pilate ..." One can reappropriate the cross by looking at it historically. Crucifixion was a deliberately cruel way of executing a non-Roman citizen who was to be made an example of because he or she was a threat to the empire. A cross is a reminder that Jesus was, indeed, a threat to the Roman empire because his message of radical egalitarianism was subversive of the empire's patronage-based, slave-supported, hierarchical system. I now see the cross as a warning and a call. The warning is that defending oppressed people is dangerous. The call is that we're supposed to do it anyway.

Supplement

The Off-Center Cross

In April 1946, a group of Universalist ministers met in a hotel room during the Universalist General Assembly in Akron, Ohio, and pooled their ideas to create a symbol to represent Universalism.[1] Among those present were Albert Zeigler, Richard Knost, Fred Harrison, and Gordon McKeeman. The result was the off-center cross. This symbol was intended to distinguish Universalism from mainstream Christianity.

Two of those present have described the symbol's significance as follows.

> The Circle is drawn to represent the all-inclusive faith of universalism which shuts no one out. In that circle is placed the cross, symbolizing the beloved faith out of which our wider insight has grown. We feel that universalism is not the product of any one cultural or religious tradition, but is in fact implicit in all the great faiths…we consider ourselves to be "Universalists of Christian descent."
>
> —Albert Zeigler, *Christian Leader,* December 7, 1946, p. 558
>
> The Circle is a symbol of infinity—a figure without beginning or end.

> The Cross is the symbol of Christianity. It is placed off-center in the circle of infinity to indicate that Christianity is an interpretation of infinity but neither the only interpretation of the infinite nor necessarily for all people, the best one. It leaves room for other symbols and other interpretations. It is, therefore, a symbol of Universalism.
>
> —Gordon McKeeman to Ronald and Jesselyn Bartlett, members of First Parish Universalist Church, Stoughton, Massachusetts, 1989

The off-center cross was used in a public service of worship for the first time on September 29, 1946, at the ordination of Earle McKinney in Foxborough, Massachusetts. The off-center cross was adopted as symbolic of Universalism in Massachusetts by the Massachusetts Universalist Convention in 1947.

Shouldn't There Be Other Symbols Too?

UUs seeing the off-center cross for the first time frequently ask, "Shouldn't there be other religious symbols, and not just the cross, in the circle of Universalism?"

The trouble is, other religious symbols are problematic for people brought up in close contact with those religious traditions, just as the cross can be for Jews and former Christians. The Taoist symbol, for example, will evoke—for someone from China—not the ancient, philosophical Taoism popular among UUs but the magical Taoism of modern China.

Also, do we want symbols on our walls that we don't really understand? Most of us have heard a sermon or two on Taoism and have perhaps read an article, but actually know relatively little about it.

The off-center cross, while expressing an openness to insights from other world religions, also acknowledges that Universalism has grown out of Christianity.

"You Should Lose the Cross."

The speaker was Mike E., an angry former Catholic visiting a UU church that had the Universalist off-center cross at the focal point of its sanctuary.

"We want to tell the truth about our denomination," replied the minister. "Historically, Christianity is the only heritage the UU movement has.

"And we also want to tell the truth about ourselves," the minister continued. "Most of us have Christian backgrounds. And while many of us came here wanting to forget about Christianity, our experience has been that it's more rewarding to learn how to take Christianity apart, discard the bad things, then incorporate the good things into our new, UU faith."

Mike E. never returned.

Does it make sense for UU churches to use the off-center cross? I think it does. Mike E. needed to get over his anger—not only for his own sake but also for that of any congregation he might join. My perception is that while a church that challenges people to address their religious pasts may thereby repel some visitors, it does a much better job of retaining those who eventually join.

The UUA Logo

I know a woman with a very Irish name—I'll call her Kerry O'Malley—who identifies strongly with her Irish heritage. She wears Celtic-knot jewelry. She has vacationed in County Kerry (her paternal grandfather's birthplace) several times, and has learned to speak a little Irish. She even has a small shamrock tattooed on one shoulder.

Kerry is three-quarters Hispanic! Yet she has never visited Puerto Rico, the birthplace of her other three grandparents. She speaks no Spanish.

The logo of the Unitarian Universalist Association (UUA) makes me think of Kerry. The flaming chalice—alas, still looking more like a birdbath than a drinking vessel—is now in the center and surrounded by rays. *This,* the logo says, represents our faith.

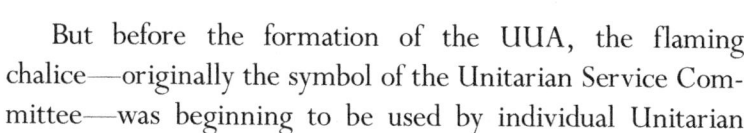

But before the formation of the UUA, the flaming chalice—originally the symbol of the Unitarian Service Committee—was beginning to be used by individual Unitarian churches as a symbol of *Unitarianism*. The UUA's previous logo, for all its problems, at least made an attempt—by placing the chalice off-center—to acknowledge that our heritage is more than Unitarianism alone. The new logo says simply: we're Unitarian. It's like Kerry's shamrock saying: I'm Irish.

But Kerry is mostly something else, as is UUism. In *The Premise and the Promise*, a history of UUism published in 2001 by the UUA, Warren Ross writes (p. 190):

> *Universalism won.* Though the Universalists were the weaker partner at the beginning, Universalism "won" in the long run—not in the sense of power, but because Unitarian Universalist values today are closer to historic Universalism than of Unitarianism.

The analogy between the flaming chalice and Kerry's tattoo breaks down in that Kerry can explain *why* the shamrock is a symbol of Ireland in a way that is simple and easy to remember. The flaming chalice cannot be explained in so straightforward a manner. The UUA Web site[2] offers no fewer than ten possible meanings and then concludes:

> There is no one official meaning of the flaming chalice. Like our faith, it stands open to new and ongoing interpretation and significance.

Why would smart people like UUs become devoted to a symbol of uncertain meaning that obscures what is apparently the more important part of their heritage?

I Discover Universalism

Kerry looks Hispanic, not Irish. Hispanic genes "won." Yet she downplays her Puerto Rican heritage because of personal history—she grew up at a time and in a place where it was much more difficult to be proud of being Puerto Rican than of being Irish.

The UU movement is likewise affected by personal history—the personal histories of the majority of UUs (lay and ordained) who have unresolved conflicts with Christianity. UUs may like a lot of things about Universalism, but Universalism itself must be allowed to disappear because it makes a specific demand that most UUs cannot abide—that the UU movement maintain contact with its Judeo-Christian roots.

The previous UUA logo can be understood as a combination of the flaming chalice and Universalism's off-center cross. The cross in the circle was replaced by the chalice, then moved to the other side. Though the resulting meaning was absurd—relativized Unitarianism?!—the important thing was to *get rid* of that cross.

Universalists agree that mainstream Christianity has been corrupted by theological nonsense, lust for power, sexism, and anti-Semitism (to name only some of its problems). But—like it or not—Christianity is the only heritage UUism has, historically, and is the only religious tradition that preserves (some of) the words and deeds of the world-class religious genius Jesus of Nazareth.

Most UUs who disown a Christian background do so because they don't know how to separate Christianity's toxic components from elements that could still nourish them. As a result, they're always spiritually hungry and suckers for the latest spiritual fad that invariably leaves them unsatisfied and susceptible to the next fad.

The 1780 Massachusetts Constitution, written by Unitarian John Adams, refers to ministers as "public protestant teachers of piety, religion and morality." I call on my fellow UU ministers—and, recognizing that it can be hard for old dogs to learn new tricks, I especially call on UU seminarians—to recommit themselves to their role as *teachers*. Teachers *shape* tastes and do not merely accommodate them. ("God and Jesus make your neck crawl because of experience in another church? Okay, we'll drop them.") I know from experience that it is possible to learn to free our Judeo-Christian roots from the tangle of poison and nonsense that threaten to suffocate them. I suggest that we ministers owe it to the UU movement to learn to do this and to pass on our skill to our congregations.

Chapter 2: Universalism in a Nutshell

God is love.
No one is condemned.
The way to be happy is to do good.
There are sources of religious truth outside the Judeo-Christian tradition.

God is love.

While Universalism, like Unitarianism, had European forebears, I think both movements are best understood as American-grown. And while Universalism has roots in Pennsylvania and New Jersey, as well as in New England, it was New Englanders who organized what became the Universalist Church of America. I will focus on them.

Universalism in New England got its start during the Revolutionary War. At that time there were few Catholics or Jews in New England, and few Native Americans still practicing their traditional faith. Most religious people were Protestants, and most Protestant preachers, embracing a harsh form of Christianity called Calvinism, were preaching hellfire. They saw God as a stern and judging god, who was going to send most people to hell forever. But a few preachers—these were the first Universalists[1]—said, "No! We don't believe in a God like that! We believe that God is a god of love, who would never cut off any of God's children."

This was not so much a reasoned conclusion as a visceral reaction. To express it, Universalists adopted the Christian saying "God is love" (from the first letter of John in the New Testament) as their very own. In their homes, they incorporated it into samplers that they hung in the parlor. In their churches, they painted it on pulpits and carved it into chancel tables. They put it on the mastheads of newsletters and the covers of orders of service.

"God is love" is the fundamental Universalist intuition.

No one is condemned.

Not even Hitler. God's love knows no bounds—it is universal. (This is how Universalists got their name.) Somehow, God finds a way to save *everybody*.

To Universalists, salvation was not a reward for good behavior but an expression of God's love. The novelty of this idea is illustrated in the following anecdote about the Universalist leader Rev. Hosea Ballou (1771–1852).

> He had gone to an inland town on a preaching engagement and had made arrangements to stay with a lady who, as it turned out, believed that men are to be saved only if they are good. Arriving at the house on Saturday afternoon, Ballou found her in the kitchen, mop in hand. Looking up, the woman said:
> "This is Mr. Ballou, I suppose?"
> "Yes, madam, my name is Ballou."

"Well, Mr. Ballou, they say you hold that all men will be saved. Do you really believe that doctrine?"

"Yes, madam, I really believe it."

"Why, sir! Do you really believe that all men are going to be saved just such creatures *as they are?*"

"What is that you have in your hand, dear woman?"

"Why," she replied, laughing, "it is my mop."

"Your mop? Well, what are you going to do with it?"

"I am going to mop up my floor. I always do it on Saturday afternoon."

"Well, sister, I understand you. Are you going to mop it up *just as it is?*"

"Mop it up just as it is?"

"Yes; you wished to know if I hold that all men will be saved *just as they are.* Do you intend to mop up the floor *just as it is?*"

"Why," she replied, "I mop it up to clean it."

"True," said Ballou. "You do not require it to be made clean before you will consent to mop it up. God saves men to purify them; that's what salvation is designed for. God does not require men to be pure in order that he may save them."[2]

While mainstream Christianity viewed God as having turned away from humanity because of human sin, Ballou's view was that it was humanity that had turned away from

God; and that God sent Jesus not to pay a price, but to remind humans of God's love.

In the twentieth century, as many Universalists moved away from traditional theism, the principle that no one is condemned was rephrased without reference to a supreme being. "We avow our faith in the supreme worth of every human personality," said the new Universalist declaration of faith (1935). In the 1980s, this was rephrased as the first of the seven Principles of the Unitarian Universalist Association.

The way to be happy is to do good.

The loving God of Universalism wants people to be happy in *this* life, too. To use Hosea Ballou's wonderful coinage, God wants to "happify" people *now*. So, God has given us such a nature that we find doing good to be deeply and lastingly satisfying.

In Universalism, the reward for doing good is not salvation in a possible next life but happiness in this one.

There are sources of religious truth outside the Judeo-Christian tradition.

Since God's love is universal (God loves *everybody*), God loves the people on the other side of the world who have never heard of Jesus or Moses, and so God sent other teachers to them—Siddhartha Gautama to India, for example, and Lao-Tzu to China. The religions they founded (Buddhism, Taoism) are also sources of religious truth.

Supplement

God Is Love

This quotation from the New Testament (1 John 4:16b) has been dear to many sects, but perhaps to none more than the Universalists. More than 200 years ago, considering it to be Biblical proof that their own understanding of God was correct, Universalists adopted it as their principal motto. In their very first declaration of faith (1790) they gave it a prominent place.

Though the Universalist view of the Bible and even God changed over the years, their conviction that God is love remained constant. They reaffirmed this commitment in their most recent declaration of faith, in 1953 (see chapter 3). Sometime around 1970, they even featured it on the badge reproduced here.[3]

Today many of us are unable to share our ancestors' faith; God is less real for us than God seems to have been for them, and for many of us, the word *God* is no more than a question mark, a name for life's mystery. At such a time, we can't help but wonder: can this vestige of an earlier age still be of use?

I say that it can. To me, "God is love" is advice for the journey. It shines light on our choice of religious paths. This venerable motto says to each of us: the experience of love can be relied on as a sign that you are headed in a right direction. It says: if the religious path you are following fosters loving relationships, then your path is a right one.

God Is Love ? !

The Universalist declaration of faith begins with an avowal of faith in God as love. What can this mean to a typical, skeptical UU who is edgy about the term *God*?

God is love?! I like it. Whoever first said this was a genius.

Notice that this ancient Christian saying doesn't seem to make sense. We are brought up to think of *God* as a person, and yet *love* is an abstract quality. How can a person be an abstract quality? Bingo! Part of the saying's message is that God *isn't* a person. God *isn't* the old man in the sky with the long white robe so many of us were brought up to believe in. "No one has ever seen God," says the biblical passage, "[but] if we love one another, God lives in us…God is love, and those who abide in love abide in God, and God abides in them."[4]

Some modern theologians have suggested that the word *God* is best understood as a *symbol*. A symbol for what is most important. A symbol for the mystery of existence. Modern theologians suggest that at the most basic level *God* is a symbol people have developed to represent the answer to the perennial questions What's the meaning of life, Why are we here, and What's it all about?

From this point of view, *God is love* offers us an answer when our hearts ask, "What's it all about?" The old saying is advising us to focus on love. We humans are small, and the universe is very big. The experience of love may be the closest we can ever come to knowing what it's all about.

Lincoln Recalls an Old Baptist

Abraham Lincoln, though very reserved about expressing his own religious views, once quoted, with apparent approval, an old Baptist who in Lincoln's youth had proclaimed at a public meeting: "When I do good, I feel good. When I do bad, I feel bad. That's my religion."

Chapter 3: Universalism and UU Renewal[1]

Renewal? The UU movement needs renewal? I think it does, and I'd like to offer three reasons why.

First, in 1961, when the denominations joined forces, there were a total of 151,557 adult UUs. Forty years later, there were 156,968 adult UUs or a net gain of less than four percent. Meanwhile the population of North America went up something like fifty percent, so as a percentage of the population, we actually declined considerably in forty years. To me that's a symptom of a need for renewal.

Second, there's a lot of talk about "spirituality" in UU churches. I think spirituality is like sex—in that it is variously understood, variously defined, variously experienced, *and* people who have enough don't spend a lot of time talking about it! I interpret the talk about spirituality as a sign of a deep-seated hunger on the part of members of our congregations, and therefore as another symptom of a need for renewal.

Third, a great many members of UU congregations are intolerant of Christianity. Some of these people are Jews, but most are traumatized former Christians. What they have in common is that they are angry with Christianity, and they are angry with Christianity because they have been hurt by it. This widespread intolerance makes our movement look ridiculous. We loudly preach tolerance, while regularly appearing to be intolerant of North America's principal religion.

We brag about our openness to world religions but often give the impression that we don't recognize Christianity as a world religion. Intolerance of Christianity is a wound at the heart of our movement, and to me, it is a third symptom of a need for renewal.

I will address only the symptoms of spiritual hunger and anti-Christianity, but in my mind these are directly related to our decline relative to the population.

I believe that a root cause of the spiritual hunger and anti-Christianity can be expressed in the phrase *turning away*. UUism makes it easy for people to turn away from big religious questions. UUism enables people to turn away from their personal religious pasts. UUism even turns away from its own religious past.

I will eventually say, of course, that a greater emphasis on Universalism is a solution to our problems. I will say that Universalism encourages people to face the big religious questions, that it helps people to confront their own religious pasts, and that it willingly acknowledges the UU movement's Christian past. But first I'd better say, in more detail, what I mean by *Universalism*.

Universalism Defined

Universalism is a popular word, and lots of UUs want to appropriate it. I have seen ministers hold up Universalist worship materials from the late nineteenth century—a time when Universalism had lost touch with its radical roots and was trying to blend in with mainline Protestantism—and declare triumphantly, "This is the real Universalism!"

I have also seen ministers reduce *Universalism* to an openness to world religions, as I believe the Rev. Forrest Church does in "Universalism: A Theology for the 21st Century," the cover story of the November-December 2001 issue of *UUWorld*.[2]

For purposes of this chapter, I will use the term *Universalism* to denote the religion described by the Universalist movement itself at the end of its independent existence. Universalism is a network of ideas evoked by the off-center cross symbol and the declaration of faith adopted by the Universalist General Assemblies of 1935 and 1953 (discussed below). This last, official Universalism is a religion that seeks to walk a knife-edge between staying in touch with its Christian heritage and staying open to insights from other religious paths.

I will say more about Universalism below, but for the moment let me return to what I see as the UU movement's principal theological problems.

Turning Away from Big Religious Questions

At the time of the consolidation of the American Unitarian Association with the Universalist Church of America (1960-61), humanism was a potent force in the Unitarian denomination. Since the Unitarians outnumbered the Universalists five to one and were bursting with confidence while the Universalists were correspondingly discouraged, the Unitarian point of view came to dominate the combined movement. As a result, humanism continues to shape UUism today. Since I'm basically a humanist myself, I'd like to begin by affirming humanism.

It is often said that *humanism* is a polite term for atheism, and that's sort of true. The "Humanist Manifesto," published in 1933 on the front page of the *Christian Register*, the Unitarian weekly newspaper, contained this phrase: "We are convinced that the time has passed for theism..." Nevertheless, to say that humanism is a polite term for atheism is not, I think, exactly true. Curtis Reese, one of the early leaders of the humanist movement, wrote, "the Humanist regards the universe as the given and is not likely to speculate unduly on either the beginning or the end of things cosmic."[3] In other words, humanism doesn't so much deny God as ignore God. The humanist attitude is that, since no adequate understanding of God has emerged from thousands of years of conventional religion, one should be practical and focus on what really matters—human life and its challenges—and redefine *religion* as concerned solely with human life.

There are good things about humanism. First, humanism is honest. Humanists are saying what they really think and really feel. The Rev. Frederick May Eliot, longtime president of the American Unitarian Association, who was not a humanist himself but who was sympathetic to humanism and felt that it had a valuable contribution to make, said "[the humanist] may not believe very much, as measured by orthodox standards, but what he does believe he believes with his whole mind."[4]

Second, humanism is courageous. Eliot again: "[Many religious people] are afraid to face the facts about their own beliefs lest they lose their faith altogether... Such people are building their faith upon the sand."[5] I think Eliot was thinking not only of people in the pews, but also the priests, ministers, and rabbis who do not subject their own beliefs to the kind of rigorous analysis they would use if they were, for example, buying a house (or even a car!). A lot of religious people wall off their beliefs in a separate mental compartment, insulating them from analysis and skepticism. It's courageous of humanists to refuse to do this.

Third, I would say humanism is correct. In thousands of years, conventional religions have not produced an adequate understanding of God. But I would add: we don't need humanism to tell us so. One of the Ten Commandments says not to make images of God; it's usually understood to mean not to make statues, but I think its wisdom is broader. We make images of God all the time, with concepts, and when those concepts prove inadequate we say we no longer believe in God, when what we actually no longer believe in are our own limited concepts.

There's one respect in which I think humanism is not as honest, courageous, or correct as it could be, and it is that humanism tends not to face the questions that conventional religions are trying to answer. Though I agree that the answers conventional religions provide are inadequate, I think that people have a deep need to face the questions anyway.

A.J. Mattill, Jr., onetime minister of Liberty Universalist Church near Louisville, Mississippi, once said: "'God' is a name my heart gives to the mystery of the universe."[6] That struck a chord with me. I thought, *"There's* a God that certainly exists. There *is* a mysteriousness about life, and that's what people are grappling with when they use the word *God."* *God* is the X of life's equation, the meaning we seek, the answer we long for. The all-too-human mistake that humanism saves us from is thinking that we *know* the answer that the name *God* represents.

The trouble is, humanism also encourages us to ignore the question. If I ignore God, as humanism encourages me to do, I'm ignoring the existence of the enormous mystery that is right in front of me. I'm born into a world I didn't create. It is very old and very big—bigger than I am, bigger than anyone, bigger than all humanity. I can't say much else about it, but awareness of this mystery enriches my life. It gives me perspective. It helps me keep my priorities straight. It deepens my experience.

In one of my favorite "Calvin and Hobbes" comic strips, Calvin and Hobbes are looking at the night sky, and Calvin is lecturing Hobbes about astronomy—that star is so many light-years away, there's the Milky Way, that kind of thing. In the second panel, the lecture continues. In the third panel, there's a brief pause. Calvin has run out of things to say, and the two friends gaze at the stars in silence. But after only a moment Calvin looks at his watch and says, "I wonder what's on TV." To me, that's what humanism encourages us to do. Of course, Calvin is going to go inside and watch cartoons. What humanism encourages us to do, once we've run out of facts, is to go inside and watch *Nova*.

Let me tell you a Bible story (1 Kings 19:11-13, New Revised Standard Version). The prophet Elijah has gone to the mountain where, hundreds of years earlier, Moses supposedly encountered God. Elijah is huddling at the back of a cave near the summit, having heard that God is about to pass by. The story continues, "Now there was a great wind, so strong that it was splitting mountains and breaking rocks in pieces...but God wasn't in the wind; and after the wind an earthquake, but God wasn't in the earthquake; and after the earthquake a fire, but God wasn't in the fire; and after the fire a sound of sheer silence. When Elijah heard it, he wrapped his face in his mantle and went out and stood at the entrance of the cave. Then there came a voice to him that said, 'What are you doing here, Elijah?'" The text doesn't say God spoke to him, it says a voice came to him. And the voice said, *"What are you doing here, Elijah?"*

I wish Calvin had lingered in the third panel. If Calvin had remained side by side with his friend Hobbes, in silence, looking out at the hugeness of space, the blackness of it, the great age of it, slack-jawed and gaping, I'm sure that within a few minutes a voice would have come to Calvin, too. He would have heard questions in his head. "What's the purpose of all this?" "What's it all about?" *"What are you doing here, Calvin?"* That's a religious experience—confrontation with the mystery of the universe, with what people mean by *God*. But that's precisely what humanism encourages us to turn away from. I don't think it's surprising that in a denomination so strongly influenced by humanism, we find widespread spiritual hunger.

Turning Away from One's Personal Religious Past

The mainstream UU movement was of no help to me while I struggled to take my childhood religion apart and then incorporate the parts that still nourished me into my adult UU faith. No minister I knew was of any help, nor any General Assembly resolution, nor any UUA publication. I fear that my experience is not unusual.

Some say that Unitarian Universalism is the gateway from Methodism to golf. I think there's a lot of truth to that. Regularly people come to our churches, are encouraged to turn their backs on their former religions and then, not finding much to stay for, leave—sometimes for another church but often, for the Sunday paper or Sunday golf. We don't encourage people to confront their religious pasts. We enable people to deny their pasts. "I was a Methodist," says a visitor. "That's nice," we say, "but come read Thoreau and Emerson and let us tell you about Buddhism and the UU Principles." While those are certainly worthy things to introduce people to, we're not helping people take their former religions apart. As a consequence, we fail to help them to reappropriate spiritual resources that, in combination with the UU perspective, would be of great value to them.

The Retreat from Religion

Visitors often comment that UUism doesn't seem like a real religion. The UU Principles, while unobjectionable, strike them as secular ("could have been written by an agency of the United Nations") and for the most part unchallenging ("Who *isn't* in favor of peace and justice?").

This state of affairs is the legacy of a bitter controversy that raged for more than 100 years, mostly in the Unitarian denomination, between liberal Christians and those further to the left—humanists and their nineteenth-century forerunners—who objected to traditional religious language (like *God*) and to the singling out of Jesus among the world's spiritual leaders. Unwilling to be split over doctrinal differences (to its everlasting credit) but seeing no alternative except to retreat from endorsing any particular religious path, the Unitarian movement came to describe itself primarily in terms of principles of procedure ("freedom, reason, tolerance") on which everyone could agree. Unitarianism became not so much a religion as a *Robert's Rules of Order* for having a discussion about religion. When the Unitarians joined forces with the much smaller Universalist movement in 1960-61, most Unitarians were unaware that the Universalists had worked out their own distinctive resolution of the Christian-humanist conflict and so the Unitarian approach prevailed. As a result, today's UUism is not so much a religion as a process that supports people who are searching for a religion. Or as one wit put it, "In UUism you're parachuted into a jungle, given a machete and a canteen, and told, 'You're free'."

While the Christian-humanist controversy was raging among Unitarians, Universalists had quietly forged their new declaration of faith (reprinted below), which is a *synthesis* of liberal Christianity and humanism. Two of the five points (supreme worth and authority of truth) embody humanist values, while the other three proclaim liberal Christianity. True to its heritage, Universalism ("the Larger Faith") had opened its arms and grown larger still.

In Universalism, you're still parachuted into a jungle, still given a machete and canteen and told that you're free, but you're also given a *compass* and shown a *direction* in which many others have found spiritual fulfillment. Universalism is more than a process; it's a religion.

The Universalist Declaration of Faith
(Washington-Andover Avowal)

We avow our faith in
 God as eternal and all-conquering love;
 the spiritual leadership of Jesus;
 the supreme worth of every human personality;
 the authority of truth, known or to be known; and
 the power of men of good will and sacrificial spirit to overcome all
 evil and progressively establish the Kingdom of God.
Neither this nor any other statement shall be imposed as a creedal test.
 —Universalist General Assemblies of 1935 and 1953

We avow our faith in God as eternal and all-conquering love. Universalism insists on using the word *God* and so confronting the big religious questions ("What am I doing here?" "What's it all about?"). By linking God with love, Universalism is suggesting that the experience of love may be the closest we can ever come to an answer.

The spiritual leadership of Jesus. Not Christ, Jesus. And not only Jesus. The importance of other religious teachers (like Moses, Buddha, and Lao-Tzu) has been acknowledged in Universalism implicitly since at least 1803 and explicitly since at least the 1820s. In 1946, the off-center cross was designed to symbolize this openness.

By singling out Jesus and by depicting only the Christian cross within its symbol, Universalism challenges the anti-Christianity of so many UUs and makes it impossible to deny the UU movement's Christian heritage. At the same time, though, the placement of the cross expresses Universalism's desire to keep its Christian heritage at arm's length. The Universalist symbol says: just as we pick and choose from other religions, we pick and choose from Christianity.

Universalism helps Jews in our congregations to see that what the UU movement chooses to keep from Christianity is mostly of Jewish origin. Universalism encourages angry former Christians to take their childhood religion apart so that it will lose its power to hurt them, freeing them to incorporate elements of Christianity that they still value into their adult faith. The result for both groups is greater spiritual depth, and healing for the UU movement as a whole.

The supreme worth of every human personality. This principle, of humanist origin, has in recent years been slightly rephrased and adopted as the first of the UU Principles.

The authority of truth, known or to be known. Universalism is committed to reason and open to new truth from whatever source.

And the power of [people] of good will and sacrificial spirit to overcome all evil and progressively establish the Kingdom of God. For Universalism, as for Jesus, the kingdom of God is here—it is a vision of the earth, finally made just.

Neither this nor any other statement shall be imposed as a creedal test. When a proviso contained in the 1935 version of this *liberty clause* was deleted in 1953, Universalism's commitment to individual freedom of belief became total.

Universalism and Religious Maturity

Much of what I've said can be summarized in terms of the *stages of faith* described by psychologist and theologian James Fowler.[7] Many UUs are at Fowler's fourth *(individuative-reflective)* stage of faith. They have demythologized the stories and symbols of their religious heritage, and they have come to express their religious convictions in terms of ethical principles and commitment to social justice. UUism does a good job of feeding people who are at this stage, but it doesn't do a good job of feeding people who are ready to move on to the next stage or who are already there. This is why there is so much spiritual hunger in our congregations.

Fowler's next (fifth) stage of faith is the one at which some of the old stories and symbols are reappropriated on a new level of understanding. I feel this is the stage I was ready to move on to when I found Universalism so helpful. Fowler calls this stage *conjunctive* because it is characterized by the acceptance of *both* parts of pairs of alternatives that were formerly perceived to be mutually exclusive. Universalism is conjunctive in this sense. It has a Declaration of Faith that is creed-like but claims not to be a creed. It embraces both sides of the Christian-humanist controversy. It proclaims its Christian roots while it relativizes Christianity as only one of the world's religious paths.

Like UUism, Universalism sustains people who are at the fourth stage of faith. But unlike UUism, Universalism also encourages people who are ready to move on from stage four to stage five (and beyond), and provides food for the journey.

At consolidation, the Unitarian majority, mistaking Universalism for an undeveloped form of their own religion instead of a distinct religion, saw no need to learn about Universalism. So, Universalism was pretty much forgotten—it was wrapped up and put in the attic, so to speak, at UUA headquarters. As a result, Universalism is now only a byway within the UU movement, trod by relatively few. But if, as I believe, the principal duty of a religious movement is to foster religious maturity among its people, then Universalism has the potential to become a highway of renewal for the entire UU movement because Universalism fosters religious maturity to a degree that UUism cannot. A solution to the UU movement's theological problems may be sitting in our own attic, fresh as the day it was put there, just waiting to be unwrapped.

Supplement

The Elephant in the Room

"There's an elephant in the room. It is large and squatting, so it is hard to get around it. Yet we squeeze by with 'How are you?' and 'I'm fine'...and a thousand other forms of trivial chatter. We talk about the weather. We talk about work. We talk about everything else—except the elephant in the room."

In Terry Kettering's poem, the elephant is a death in her family. In many UU churches, the elephant is Christianity. A majority of Unitarian Universalists—including a majority of our ministers—have unresolved conflicts with Christianity. There is a need, therefore, to talk about Christianity. We need to take it apart, distinguish its varieties, jettison what is not useful, and keep what is. We need to do this, but mostly we do not.

"There's an elephant in the room," the poem continues. "We all know it is there. We are thinking about the elephant as we talk together. It is constantly on our minds. For, you see, it is a very big elephant...But we do not talk about the elephant in the room."

Universalism helps UUs to talk about the elephant in the room. Indeed, the Universalist symbol and declaration of faith make such a discussion unavoidable. This is one reason the UU movement needs to stay in touch with the Universalist side of its heritage.

"Oh, please, let's talk about the elephant in the room," says the poet. "Can I [speak of it] to you and not have you look away? For if I cannot, then you are leaving me alone…in a room…with an elephant."

Bringing Jesus Out the Door with Them

—Dave Johnson, El Paso, Texas

Many people have fled the Christianity in which they grew up. But if you quiz them, you'll find something interesting: few of them left Jesus behind. They brought him out the door with them.

They walked away from Paul's Greek *mystery*. They walked away from the politics of imperialism that manifests itself even today as *religious authority*. They walked away from *belief in* God. They walked away from worshipping *Jesus Christ*. They walked away from being rejected on account of personal characteristics (for instance homosexual orientation or an inability to tolerate superstition). They walked away from the church's refusal to accept the disciplines of modern science or of truthful history. They walked away from preachers' and bishops' refusal to take responsibility for what they teach and to teach "as one[s] having authority," as Jesus did.

But the Jesus who taught truth not as dogma but as a way of life produced by the discipline of honesty is a welcome companion on their spiritual journey in the wilderness.

Also Free to Keep

Some newcomers to UU congregations, elated that they are not asked to subscribe to a fixed creed and exhilarated by their freedom to discard outworn doctrines, can be so boisterous in their religious housecleaning as to give other newcomers the impression that in UU congregations people are expected to completely reject their religious pasts and start over from scratch. It isn't true. UUism has no concept of conversion.

It's a fact that because we are creedless, there's nothing you *have to* embrace in a UU congregation. But by the same token, there's nothing you have to shed. You are free, yes, to discard everything from your religious past that is no longer valuable to you. But at the same time, you are also free to keep everything that still nourishes you. Becoming *UU* doesn't mean you stop being *you*.

One Mountain, One Special Path

In his marvelous book *Finding Your Religion,* the Rev. Scotty McLennan tells of his encounter with a Hindu Brahmin priest and the Hindu concept of *one mountain, many paths*. Scotty's initial reaction was that of many UUs: "Maybe this is the way to spiritual maturity. Be open to all religious traditions. Pick and choose what rings true for me in each."[8]

The Hindu priest objected. "There are many paths up the mountain and they all reach the top, but…you can't be on more than one at a time." He advised, "You've grown up as a Christian and you know a lot about that path... Go back and be the best Christian you can be."

"But I don't believe Jesus was any more divine than Krishna or the Buddha," protested Scotty. "And Christians would condemn you for knowing about Jesus and not accepting him uniquely as your Lord and Savior."

"Then go back and find a way to be an open, nonexclusive Christian," said the priest, adding that the more Scotty could learn about others' paths, the more it would help him to progress along his own.

The priest was counseling Universalism. Universalism is an interfaith religion that seeks not to lose touch with the UU movement's Christian roots. Its symbol, a circle with off-center cross, can be viewed as a mountain seen from above. Though the religion of Jesus is only one path to the summit, we single it out because it is the path of our heritage.

Humanists for Jesus

UUs widely assume that Universalists are Christians. While many Universalists are, many others might be more accurately described as humanists for Jesus. It saddens me to feel that I have to make this distinction, but I've noted that while many UUs may tolerate and even welcome a person they have categorized as Christian, they will pay little attention to what the person says. I want to be heard.

So who are humanists for Jesus? We're humanists. We ignore questions about the supernatural and think that religion should focus on human life and its problems. We assume that Jesus is dead as a doornail. But we also think that Jesus was a world-class religious genius, on a par with Buddha and Lao-Tzu, and that he should certainly be commended to the attention of UUs who, despite their professed interest in world religions, are estranged from the only religious tradition that preserves some of his words and deeds.

Other Things Universalism Has to Offer

In this chapter, I've spoken of Universalism's power to bring healing to individual UUs who have unresolved conflicts with Christianity, and its power, by so doing, to bring healing to the UU movement as a whole. I'd like to mention two other things Universalism has to offer.

First, Universalism helps attract the never-churched. In recent years, another group of people have been visiting UU churches in significant numbers—people we might call the *never-churched*. These people are not refugees from other religions but come to us with no formal religious background at all. They are looking for something beyond what the secular world has to offer and are unencumbered by old religious traumas.

To these visitors, the UUA logo—a flaming chalice—is not recognizable as a religious symbol. And when they read the seven UU Principles, though they agree with every one, they don't recognize them as religious. The seven

Principles could have been written by a secular organization like an agency of the United Nations; they don't *feel* religious.

The off-center cross, in contrast to the UUA logo, is immediately identifiable as a religious symbol because it incorporates the widely recognized symbol of the cross. And the Universalist declaration of faith feels like a religious statement because of its use of biblical language. Though it expresses the same values as the seven Principles, it does so in a way that is recognizably religious.

Second, Universalism helps attract people from less privileged social classes. We UUs say we want to be *everybody's* church. We speak of the inherent worth and dignity of every person. We say we want our congregations to be welcoming. We are heartbroken that our movement includes so few people of color. We say we wish there were more people in our congregations who work with their hands or are paid by the hour.

We *say* we want to be everybody's church, yet our language is wrong. Mainstream UUism—the UUism of UUA publications—doesn't speak the language of the majority of religious people in North America. To the average person, UUism is too "weird."

Universalism, on the other hand, was shaped by the experience of less privileged people, and so it speaks to the average person. Despite differences in ethnicity and social class, most North Americans who are brought up to be religious are brought up in religions that involve the Bible. Universalism speaks the language of this majority—though in a challenging, new way.

Just by speaking the language, Universalism conveys that if you come to a UU church, you don't have to give up everything. UU values are compatible with much of your tradition. But by using the language in a new way, Universalism also conveys that if you come to a UU church, you do have to *reevaluate* everything. We are not religion as usual!

Rev. Lovejoy on UUism

>—"I'm Goin' to Praiseland," *The Simpsons*,
> original air date May 6, 2001

[The Simpson family is attending a church ice cream social.]

Lisa: Wow, look at all these flavors! Blessed Virgin Berry, Command-Mint, Bible Gum?

Rev. Lovejoy: Or, if you prefer, we also have Unitarian [Universalist] ice cream. [Hands Lisa an empty bowl.]

Lisa: There's nothing here.

Rev. Lovejoy: Exactly.

Universalism for Young People

The following young people's version of the Universalist declaration of faith is by the Rev. Dr. Elizabeth M. Strong.

I believe:
God is love
Jesus is a teacher and a friend
In the goodness of people
There is truth I know and more I will know
Service is required of me to live my faith, and
In the end all will be well.

Chapter 4: "What's the Difference between Universalism and Unitarianism?"

Newcomers to Unitarian Universalist congregations often ask this question. Recently the distinction has become quite blurred, but in the early days there were clear differences between the two groups. (There is further discussion in chapter 6.)

• In America Universalism is the older movement, by thirty to forty years. What became the Universalist Church of America was founded in 1793; the original American Unitarian Association, in 1825.

• In New England, Universalism developed mainly in the hill country of central New England, an area that was then frontier. Unitarianism developed in long-established settlements around Boston.

• Universalists were generally from a less-privileged social class than Unitarians. Hosea Ballou, who was the principal Universalist leader for more than forty years, was born in a log cabin in Richmond, New Hampshire, and had less than two years' formal education. William Ellery Channing, his Unitarian counterpart, was born to an aristocratic family in Newport, Rhode Island, and was sent to Harvard.

• Universalism developed among lay people. Unitarianism originated among Harvard-educated clergy.

- The first Universalists were *come outers* who walked out of their home congregations and started new, liberal congregations. In this way their experience was like that of many UUs today. The first Unitarians were *stay inners* whose congregations were gradually guided by their ministers into a liberal direction.

- Universalists had to build their own new meetinghouses. Unitarians inherited buildings that had been built by the town and were maintained at public expense.

- While both religions championed the use of reason and individual freedom of belief, their basic viewpoints were very different. Unitarian minister Thomas Starr King, son of a Universalist minister, famously explained the difference with an anecdote about a Universalist minister who summarized a dispute with a Unitarian minister in these words: "The Universalist...believes that God is too good to damn us forever; and you Unitarians believe that you are too good to be damned."[1]

The Unitarians saw the moral realm as they saw society—stratified, with some people successful and others not. Their slogan, *Salvation by character*, meant that those who succeed in developing a high moral character will be saved while those who do not succeed will be condemned. By regarding salvation as something that one earns by doing good, Unitarians were adopting a view similar to that of Catholics and Methodists, for example, though these denominations drew mostly from lower social classes and the Unitarians did not regard them as peers.

The Universalists had a more egalitarian view that was expressed provocatively by Hosea Ballou as "salvation irrespective of character."[2] Salvation was not earned; it was a gift to all from a God whose nature is love. And people who do evil things are not so much evil as uninformed. They have not yet realized that the path to happiness in *this* life is doing good.

Supplement

The Winchester Profession

The Washington-Andover Avowal, which I used in chapter 3 to define Universalism, gives only one snapshot of Universalist theology. For a more comprehensive view we should also examine the much earlier (1803) Winchester Profession, which was never repealed and was understood to be included in all later declarations of faith.[3] The Winchester Profession may seem old-fashioned at first, but in some ways, it is more radical.

Universalist congregations began forming in New England in the late 1770s. By 1794, they extended from Long Island Sound to central Vermont and New Hampshire, and from the Atlantic to Lake Champlain.[4] The majority were in the hill country of central Massachusetts, southern New Hampshire, and southern Vermont. Winchester, New Hampshire is at the center of this region. It was in the meetinghouse there that Universalists gathered in 1803 to ratify the declaration of faith that came to be known as the Winchester Profession.

The Winchester Profession served Universalists for almost a century. It is the grandparent of the Washington-Andover Avowal and the great-great-grandparent of the seven Principles of the Unitarian Universalist Association.

The Winchester Profession

Article I. We believe that the Holy Scriptures of the Old and New Testaments contain a revelation of the character of God, and of the duty, interest and final destination of mankind.

Article II. We believe that there is one God, whose nature is Love, revealed in one Lord Jesus Christ, by one Holy Spirit of Grace, who will finally restore the whole family of mankind to holiness and happiness.

Article III. We believe that holiness and true happiness are inseparably connected, and that believers ought to be careful to maintain order and practice good works; for these things are good and profitable unto men.

The Winchester Profession begins, "We believe that the Holy Scriptures of the Old and New Testaments contain a revelation of the character of God, and of the duty, interest, and final destination of [hu]mankind." Within this endorsement of the Bible, which is typical of the time, we find two crucial words signaling that Universalism was something new. One of these words is the smallest one: *a*. *We believe that the Holy Scriptures of the Old and New Testaments contain* a *revelation...* Not the unique revelation but a revelation, one revelation among many. The Judeo-Christian religious tradition isn't the only religious tradition. There are others, and they may be of value, too. It is this openness to insights from other religions that led Universalists in the twentieth century to symbolize their religion by the off-center cross (see chapter 1).

The second crucial word is also inconspicuous: *contain*. *[T]he Holy Scriptures... **contain** a revelation...* The Bible itself is not a revelation; it *contains* a revelation. Some parts of the Bible are religiously important, but other parts are not. How can these parts be distinguished? By people, using their hearts and minds. In the final analysis, each person is his or her own religious authority.

The Winchester Profession continues, "We believe that there is one God, whose nature is love..." Universalists adopted the biblical motto *God is love* as their very own.

Universalists believed that this loving God would somehow find a way to save all people—"the whole family of [hu]mankind." Universalists believed that *everyone* winds up in heaven. As we have seen, this belief, which theologians call *universal salvation*, is what gave Universalists their name. God's love is universal, they said. God loves everybody.

Many were scandalized by this. They asked, without the threat of eternal hellfire, why should people be good? In several states, Universalists were barred from serving on juries or testifying as witnesses because it was presumed that a Universalist would have no motive to be honest. With characteristic originality, Universalists replied, "We believe that

holiness and true happiness are inseparably connected..."
People should be good and do good, they said, because God
has given us such a nature that we find it fulfilling to so conduct ourselves. Doing good is how to be happy in *this* life.

Appended to the Winchester Profession was a so-called *liberty clause*, affirming the freedom of Universalist congregations to add their own particular beliefs to the denominational profession. In later declarations of faith, Universalists enlarged this liberty clause until, in 1953, it affirmed complete freedom of belief for every individual: *Neither this nor any other statement shall be imposed as a creedal test.*

Misplacing Our History

It happens like this: someone describes an episode from Universalist history as *Unitarian Universalist*. Then someone else shortens that to *Unitarian*, and the result is that a part of Universalist history is now remembered as Unitarian. Not long ago, for example, I heard someone refer to the battle for separation of church and state in Massachusetts (not won until 1833!) as having been "Unitarian-led." It was Universalists in Gloucester who began that fight in 1781. Unitarians did not even begin to emerge on the religious scene until about 1805; once they did, they were by and large *opposed* to separation because *their* churches (founded much earlier) were beneficiaries of the old system. To speak of the fight for separation as "Unitarian-led" is ludicrous.

To prevent such distortions, I urge *all* UUs to insist that the term *Unitarian Universalist* never be used to describe events that occurred before 1960-61 (when the denominations joined forces), and that the term never be shortened to *Unitarian* (use *UU* instead).

What is at stake is more than the sensibilities of a few self-styled Universalists. If the Universalist perspective is forgotten, our combined UU movement will suffer an irretrievable loss.

The MLK-Universalist Connection

In the season of Dr. Martin Luther King Jr. Day and Black History Month many UU preachers remind their congregations of the connection between King and Thoreau, who was a (nominal) Unitarian. But there's another connection between King and UUism that is less well-known and less direct but more substantial: King-Gandhi-Tolstoy-Adin Ballou.

King was inspired by the Indian freedom fighter Mohandas Gandhi, who was inspired by the religious writings of Russian novelist Leo Tolstoy, with whom Gandhi corresponded, at the end of Tolstoy's life. Tolstoy was inspired by the writings of Universalist minister Adin Ballou, with whom Tolstoy corresponded, at the end of Ballou's life.

Adin Ballou, a distant cousin of Universalist leader Hosea Ballou, was born in 1803, the year the Winchester Profession was adopted. He was a pacifist, socialist, abolitionist, and founder of the utopian community of Hopedale, Massachusetts.

We Need *All* Our History

Most UUs know little about Universalist history. This is primarily because most of our ministers—the principal transmitters of UU history—themselves know little about the Universalist side. This, in turn, is primarily because the UU history courses our ministers take in seminary often resemble the one I took in the early 1990s.

The course began by following Universalism from its American origins in the 1700s until about 1805, the year that marks the start of the "Unitarian controversy" and the emergence of the Unitarians from the old churches of eastern Massachusetts. At that point, the course's focus shifted to Unitarianism, where it remained, *exclusively*, until 1960-61, when Universalists were mentioned one final time (but only in passing), as the group with whom the Unitarians combined to form the Unitarian Universalist Association.

What brings this to mind is the UU movement's 2003 celebration of one bicentennial and virtual neglect of another.

The Emerson bicentennial was an "official" UU observance, supported by the UUA Board of Trustees. Almost $50,000 was raised and spent on high-quality and well-designed materials and events, including an exhibit, a Web site, books, a major program at General Assembly, and an array of educational and worship resources that were sent to each congregation. I have to wonder how beneficial all the extra attention given Emerson was to the UU movement. Weren't most of our ministers already referring to Emerson on a regular

"What's the Difference between Universalism and Unitarianism?"

basis? Didn't Emerson already have a secure place in our religious education curricula?

Meanwhile, a relative handful lovingly observed the bicentennial of Adin Ballou. Though he admittedly had less effect on the wider American culture than Emerson, Adin Ballou certainly deserves more recognition within the UU movement. Emerson served as one of our ministers for three years; Ballou, for fifty-six. When Emerson differed with the leaders of his church over a point of theology (communion), he resigned; when Ballou differed with the leaders of his *denomination* over a point of theology (punishment in the afterlife), he argued long and hard (and his position eventually prevailed). Emerson paid visits to a utopian community (Brook Farm); Ballou *founded* a utopian community (Hopedale).

Adin Ballou was also one of our nation's leading theorists of nonviolent resistance, directly influencing Tolstoy and through him, Gandhi. Surely, in a time of distressing belligerence by the United States, UUs would have benefited from learning about Adin Ballou. It is regrettable that the opportunity presented by his bicentennial was missed.

We UUs need *all* our history. It shapes our sense of who we are and our vision for the future.

Universalists Leading the Way: Child Dedications

The old canard that Universalists were backward Unitarians is reinforced when modern UUs read Unitarian historical material in the innocent expectation that they will hear about both sides. For example, in *Channing, the Reluctant Radical* by Jack Mendelsohn (Boston: Skinner House, 1995), we read (p. 143) that in 1818, the Unitarian leader came to propose a new interpretation of the ancient rite of baptism.

> Why baptize a child, he asked, before the child can understand or want it?... He preferred to think of the rite as pointing its primary meaning toward parents, reminding them of the "great ends for which a human life is given."

Channing's modified baptism is recognizable as what UUs now call a *child dedication*, and the reader can easily infer that Channing originated the current custom. However, John Murray, the Universalist leader, anticipated Channing by thirty-six years and even used the term *dedication*.

With the practice of dedicating children, as with so many other features of the UU movement, it was Universalists who led the way.

Universalists Leading the Way: Children's Sunday

The first Children's Sunday was celebrated at the Universalist Church of Chelsea, Massachusetts, in 1856. It was the brainchild of their minister, Charles Leonard (1822–1918), who later served as dean of the (Universalist) Divinity School at Tufts University. Its purpose, as now, was to recognize the importance of the young people in a congregation.

The idea of Children's Sunday spread quickly to other Universalist churches, and before long, some Unitarian churches adopted the custom as well. Since the two denominations joined forces in 1960-61, Children's Sunday has become an annual observance in the majority of UU churches. The traditional date is the second Sunday in June.

Universalists Leading the Way: Christmas

This is an excerpt from *The Battle for Christmas* by Stephen Nissenbaum (Vintage, 1997, pp. 45–46).

> With the turn of the nineteenth century, the re-appropriation of Christmas [by Protestants in New England] took on a concerted form—a move to hold church services on December 25. This move was led by both evangelicals and liberals. In the forefront of the evangelicals were the Universalists. Largely a rural sect, Universalists openly celebrated Christmas from the earliest stages of their existence in New England. The Universalist community in Boston held a special Christmas Day service in [1785], even before their congregation was officially organized, and in the early nineteenth century it was this denomination that proselytized for Christmas more actively than any other.
>
> The Unitarians were close behind. Compared with Universalists, Unitarians were more

genteel, and (for all their theological liberalism) more socially conservative...Unitarians were calling for the public observance of Christmas by about [1810]...in the hope that their own observance might help to purge the holiday of its associations with seasonal excess and disorder.

Universalists Leading the Way: Antislavery

While UU folklore has it that we were leaders in the movement to end slavery, the record is actually mixed. It's true that a number of Unitarians, like the ministers William Ellery Channing and Theodore Parker, were in the forefront of the antislavery cause. Most Unitarians were less outspoken because prominent members of Unitarian congregations had business interests that depended on the labor of slaves, and in the South, some Unitarians and Universalists actually owned slaves. On balance, though, both Unitarians and Universalists did much to further the antislavery cause, and, as in so many other matters, it was Universalists who led the way.

Universalists passed an antislavery resolution at the Convention of 1790 (Philadelphia), which was adopted four years later by the New England Convention (Oxford, Massachusetts). By 1794, therefore, the entire Universalist denomination had gone on record as opposing slavery, making them only the second denomination (after the Quakers) to do so. (After taking their antislavery stand the Quakers, too, had slave owners in their ranks for many decades.) By contrast, Channing's first antislavery sermon was not delivered until at least thirty-one years later, and the Unitarian denomination never went on record as opposing slavery.

Universalists Leading the Way: Unitarianism!

UUs widely assume (isn't it obvious?) that Unitarian preachers were the first in New England to preach *unitarianism*, which is essentially the doctrine that Jesus isn't God. It's not true. Almost all Universalist preachers were preaching unitarianism by 1805, at which time the people who would eventually be called *Unitarians* had not yet separated from the Congregationalists or accepted the Unitarian name. Universalists were preaching unitarianism before Unitarians existed.

Universalists had dibs on the Unitarian name! But they already had another name that they liked better.

Universalists Leading the Way: Women's Ordination

A dozen miles southeast of downtown Boston, in Weymouth, there is a small parking lot at the corner of Washington and Prospect Streets, across from a Dunkin' Donuts. The original meeting house of the First Universalist Society stood there from 1839 until it was destroyed by fire in 1938. Every time I drive by, I glance at the lot, and in my mind's eye, I see a historical marker. "Early Woman Minister," it announces and then explains, "Universalist Olympia Brown, second woman to achieve full ministerial standing in any denomination in the United States, served here 1864-69." (The first such woman, Lydia Ann Jenkins, was Universalist, too.)

With the site currently owned by the Roman Catholic Archdiocese of Boston and even discussion of women's ordination prohibited by the Vatican, I don't expect to see a marker installed any time soon. Looming over the tiny lot is huge Sacred Heart Church. Unlike the Universalist building that once stood next door, it is not owned by the people who worship there. It, too, is owned by the archdiocese.

But the archdiocese doesn't own the people. Despite the call for silence, women's ordination is frequently discussed among Catholics, and there is a large majority who are now in favor of it. A priest I knew for the last eighteen years of his life, who grew up in Sacred Heart Parish, began his career strongly opposed to women's ordination but ended it strongly in favor.

I am convinced that, unless the Catholic Church disintegrates like the Soviet Union, the day will eventually come when there are female Catholic priests. One day the pastor of Sacred Heart may be a woman. If that day comes, I hope that, as she is showing a new female curate around, the pastor's sense of sisterhood will outweigh her sectarianism, and she will point to the tiny parking lot and say excitedly, "This is where Olympia Brown, the early woman minister, served!" If that day comes, it won't matter whether the site has a marker.

Universalist Decline

In 1861, Universalists were one of America's largest denominations, many times larger than the Unitarian denomination. But by 1961, Universalists had shrunk to a tiny denomination, outnumbered by the always-small Unitarian denomination five to one.

One reason for Universalism's decline was that its distinctiveness was blurred when other denominations began to downplay hellfire and emphasize God's love. Churchgoers made a calculation: "Why should I go to the Universalist church when I can go to another, more socially prominent church, where the theological message is practically the same?"

Another reason for Universalism's decline had to do with Universalists' fear of centralized authority. In 1792, Universalists in Newport, Rhode Island, were reported to be reluctant even to meet with each other for Sunday worship, for fear of the ecclesiastical structure that they felt would inevitably follow from holding regular meetings. (And some say that Unitarian Universalists *today* have a problem with authority!) To the very end of its independent existence, the Universalist denomination never allowed its national organization to have significant authority.

Another reason may have been Universalists' enthusiasm for experimental spirituality, especially the mid-nineteenth century rage, spiritualism, or belief in the possibility of communication with the dead. "Universalists ... were quite disproportionately drawn to this belief," writes John Buescher in *The Other Side of Salvation* (Boston: Skinner House, 2003, p. viii), "and no denomination lost more of its leaders to it."

Yet another reason for Universalist decline was that, as Universalists made their way up the socioeconomic ladder, they deemphasized the most radical parts of their message in order to blend in with mainstream Protestantism. Like the Unitarians before them, they began to speak of salvation as more a matter of character-development than as a loving God's unconditional gift to every person. Universalists began to see a person's worth and dignity as being earned by individual accomplishment rather than being an inherent birthright.

Universalism experienced a theological rebirth in the decades flanking World War II. The new Washington-Andover Avowal incorporated humanist values, and a new generation of leaders reconnected Universalism to its radical roots. But these reforms came too late. When the Unitarians and Universalists combined in 1960-61, Universalism sank from sight, overwhelmed by the huge Unitarian majority. Eighty-three percent of the new Unitarian Universalists were former Unitarians who tended to ignore Universalism, mistaking it for an undeveloped form of their own religion, instead of a distinct liberal religion with its own contribution to make.

Snubbed

We have mentioned several reasons why the average UU today knows little about Univeralism:

- At consolidation, Unitarians outnumbered Universalists five to one;

- Universalists at the time tended not to emphasize the most radical elements of their religion, namely

"What's the Difference between Universalism and Unitarianism?"

Salvation *irrespective* of character and Doing good is the way to be happy *now*;

- Unitarians tended to assume that Universalism was merely an undeveloped form of their own religion and so did not warrant investigation;

- The Universalist seminaries were closed.

To this list we must add another reason: in the early days of the Unitarian denomination, most of its leaders deliberately ignored—snubbed—the Universalists. As a result, people studying the history of American Unitarianism never have their attention drawn to Universalism—it's as if Universalism never existed.

Part of the reason for the snub was that Universalism was so radical. In his autobiography Adin Ballou remembered Unitarianism's early days as follows:

> A large majority of the Unitarians at that time [1820s and 1830s] had a great dislike, amounting almost to contemptuous disgust, towards Universalists...They insisted that though some mild form of endless punishment might or might not be true, the Bible, in their opinion, did not teach universal restoration but left the final destiny of the wicked in hopeless obscurity. Moreover, they generally believed that this obscurity was wholesome in its moral and religious influence upon mankind. Therefore,

duty and expediency required them to preach the promises and threatenings of the sacred record according to the letter of the text as traditionally understood...at the same time explaining away or ignoring the letter of texts that plainly favored the doctrine of [Universalism]. In this state of opinion, they deemed it sufficiently burdensome to defend their own special Unitarian tenets against the denunciations of the self-styled orthodox sects without fathering other heresies. And they were very sensitive about being charged by their theological enemies with any leanings toward Universalism.[5]

Another factor is that between the Unitarians and the Universalists there was a chasm of social class. Adin Ballou explains:

> The Unitarians were largely a well educated class of people, and nursed the pride of having a highly educated ministry. But [Universalist preachers], tried by their standard, were "unlearned and ignorant"—only a trifle better schooled, perhaps, than the humble Nazarene himself and his original twelve apostles, without a D.D. [Doctor of Divinity] among them, and little better than barbarians when compared with the graduates of Harvard College, and other polished literati.[6]

"What's the Difference between Universalism and Unitarianism?"

Ernest Cassara, biographer of *Hosea* Ballou, speculates that:

> This social cleavage, while not mentioned openly at the time, may explain the refusal of the Unitarian ministers to exchange pulpits with the Universalists. [Hosea] Ballou favored pulpit exchanges among men of all shades of opinion represented in Boston at the time... He believed this was a way of promoting truth and eliminating error. The Unitarians, however, exchanged pulpits with Congregationalists, Baptists and other orthodox sects, but very seldom with Universalists.[7]

When "Unitarian Christianity," the epochal sermon by Unitarian leader William Ellery Channing, was published in 1819, Hosea Ballou reprinted long excerpts in *Universalist Magazine*, together with his own generally favorable assessment. Ballou was pleased that the Unitarians had finally declared their independence from the Calvinism of the Congregational churches. Ballou had hopes of becoming personally acquainted with Channing, but Channing "held himself aristocratically aloof from such a common person."[8]

The ironies are numerous. Hosea Ballou and William Ellery Channing were the leaders of the Universalist and Unitarian denominations. In 1960-61, their denominations would combine. In 1935, the churches they served would combine. For twenty-five years (1817–1842) they were both in Boston. Their churches were separated by only a few blocks. Their houses were separated by only a few blocks. In Cambridge's Mount Auburn Cemetery, their graves are separated by only a few blocks! Yet, they seem never to have become personally acquainted.

Theodore Parker on Universalism

The Rev. Robert W. Haney of the Theodore Parker Church, West Roxbury, Massachusetts, sent me the following excerpt from a letter dated June 14, 1847, from Unitarian minister Theodore Parker to his colleague the Rev. Samuel J. May of Lexington (emphasis original):

> The Universalists are more <u>human</u> than we; they declare the <u>Fatherhood of God</u> and do not stick at the consequences. <u>Everlasting Happiness to all men</u>. I think they are the most <u>human</u> sect in the land.

CHAPTER 5: UNIVERSALIST CULTURE

Some Leftovers Feed the Soul

—William J. Hamilton III
from *The Universalist Herald,* January 1993
(edited by Richard Trudeau)

When my wife and I arrived at the Red Hill Universalist Church [near Clinton, North Carolina] Saturday Night Potluck, I assumed from the terrific amount of country food that at least a hundred people were expected. I did not expect to take any of my rice bread home.

The twenty-five stalwart members that did appear, several past their fiftieth year of church membership, ate heartily. We were greeted warmly and given a thorough tour of the little brick church and yard. Before eating, they said grace. Afterwards, they talked. There was no liberal arrogance, no trendy correctness, no exaggerated sensitivity. On the still July evening, there was no hurry.

In the city churches I visit, the meat runs out early and the fried chicken doesn't last. Slim pickings await the latecomer. At Red Hill, a henhouse of drumsticks greets the last person in line.

* * *

Red Hill was founded in 1884 by the Rev. D.B. Clayton, who spent sixty-eight years preaching Universalism to the

American South. After being excommunicated by the Baptists, he spent his life sustaining the little Universalist churches he spread across the countryside with his unfailing faith that *all* would be saved. In 1886, he traveled 13,314 miles, many by horse and carriage, to deliver that message of *universal salvation*.

Once a torrential rain delayed and threatened to prevent his preaching at a little town called Freedonia Crossroads, South Carolina, forty-five miles from his home in Columbia. He went to sleep on Saturday night with a flood beating down on his roof. At midnight, when the clouds broke and moonlight filled the countryside, he got up and began a fourteen-and-a-half-hour struggle with horse and carriage over quagmire roads and swollen streams. Despite his best efforts, he arrived at 2:30 p.m. for a service planned for 11:00 a.m. Who was still waiting, three and a half hours after the time appointed for the service? The entire congregation—waiting anxiously, though patiently. He said, "I've come a long way, and I'm gonna preach a long time." He preached for an hour and a half.

What sustained Rev. Clayton through the fourteen-and-a-half-hour struggle to preach to Freedonia Crossroads, and what moved the congregation to wait for him, was a faith, grounded in an understanding of the Bible, that the love of God was more powerful than any force in the universe.

Rev. Clayton defended that faith with all his strength. Whenever news reached him from one of his congregations that a missionary had arrived in town who was preaching hellfire, Clayton would rush to that town, Bible and notes in hand, to challenge his rival to public theological debate. It was not uncommon for these debates to go on for several days.

* * *

When the Red Hill potluck ended, the members offered each other the leftovers to take home. There was enough to feed many more people. Red Hill could have fed you that evening—and you would have been welcome.

Today no faithful Universalist congregation waits at Freedonia Crossroads. Many of our rural churches are fading as the towns that surround them disappear. Perhaps that is why so much food is brought to the potlucks, to feed and strengthen what remains and the memory of what has been.

These Universalists have been waiting for decades to share a faith and a measure of love with our denomination. While these churches remain, you should visit them. If you do not like what you hear—if it is too conservative—you will value what you feel. The spirit that loads the tables—the spirit that sent Rev. Clayton across the land and held the congregation that waited on him—is there still. There are leftovers there to bring back to our city churches. The Universalist spirit will load your plate and fill your soul.

Universalist Chutzpah

Hosea Ballou, leader of the Universalist denomination for the first half of the nineteenth century, was in his younger days a "circuit rider," spending long hours on horseback traveling from town to town to preach the Universalist gospel. One day he was riding with a Baptist circuit rider who happened to be headed in the same direction, and the two passed the time in friendly theological debate.

The Baptist was flabbergasted to learn that Universalists didn't believe in a God who would condemn people to eternal hellfire. "Why, if I were a Universalist," the Baptist said, "I could knock you over the head, ride off with your money and horse, and have nothing to worry about!"

"If you were a Universalist," replied Ballou, "the thought would never occur to you."

Coffee Hour
(A Note to the UU Church of Weymouth, Massachusetts, a Universalist-Heritage Congregation)

"Do you have communion?" visitors sometimes ask, knowing that Unitarian Universalism has Christian roots. If the question comes during coffee hour, I gesture around the room. "This is communion," I say. I'm not being flip. When Jesus was alive, he and his friends ate and drank and socialized with *everyone*. After he died, his followers continued to do this, but over time the original relaxed, egalitarian gatherings evolved into something very different—formal ceremonies held during religious services, from which outsiders were excluded! UU coffee hours are like the *original* communions—separate from the religious service (and so protected from clerical meddling), informal, and welcoming.

I visit a lot of UU churches as a guest preacher—more than twenty-five in the Ballou Channing District alone—and the UU Church of Weymouth has the best coffee hour I've ever seen. You have a wonderful space—not dark or dank, like so many church basements. You have a *lot* of food. And you *sit down,* giving people a chance to really visit with one another. It's wonderful.

The Ten Commandments Revisited

—The Rev. Patrick O'Neill

My friend Heather Clayton is a fourth-generation UU. Her great-grandmother was Julia Pope Ames Fuller, a Universalist born in 1865 in Machias, Maine. A few years ago, among the family treasures, Heather found this list of the Ten Commandments as her great-grandmother first learned them in Universalist Sunday school.

1. Worship One God, Who only is good.
2. Bow to no idols of stone or of wood.
3. Speak not of God in careless ways.
4. Try to make Sunday the best of days.
5. Father and Mother, love and obey.
6. Hate not God's children, hurt not nor slay.
7. Pure be in thought and in word and in deed.
8. Keep your life free from stealing and greed.
9. Speak the truth always, never tell lies.
10. And look not on others with envious eyes.

You can tell a lot about our Universalist forebears from this list. The imperious, forbidding tone of the voice on

Mount Sinai is absent here. Instead, there is a simpler, gentler intonation expressing a theology of common sense conduct and harmonious living. Amidst the harsher Calvinistic overtones of nineteenth-century American Protestantism, this Universalist gentleness was a breath of fresh air. It is a lovely part of our UU heritage that I hope we never lose. Pass it on...

Giving a Different Kind of Finger

An index finger pointing upward. I had encountered it the year before in eastern North Carolina, carved on the nineteenth-century headstone of (male) Universalist missionary Hope Bain. The message seemed to be, "I'm in heaven," which served not only as a reassurance to loved ones, but also as a final proclamation of the nineteenth-century Universalist faith that eventually *everyone* goes there.

Now, here was the finger again, on three century-old headstones in a Universalist cemetery on a hilltop in northeast Pennsylvania. It was early on a raw and windy Sunday morning in the fall of 1997, and I had come up alone to visit the graves and study the view.

There are no Unitarian graves in those hills. Unitarianism, an ethnic religion of transplanted New Englanders, tended to hop from city to city, but Universalism sent missionaries into the countryside, where it spread like wildfire.

Universalism's message was one everyone could understand, and Universalism spoke to the heart. God is a loving god, it said, who will somehow find a way to save everybody.

We're all in the same boat, and there's nothing to fear after death. Religion is about learning to accept love, and loving, in *this* life.[1] It was an optimistic message, fittingly represented by that cheery finger pointing up. It is a message that the world still needs today.

Universalism and Class Diversity

Most of the early Universalist churches in Massachusetts were founded in the late 1700s in the hill country of the central part of the state (an area that until then was sparsely populated) by middle-class people who had withdrawn from Congregational or Baptist churches. Because of their founders' middle-class tendency toward egalitarianism, their independent-mindedness, the frontier setting, and the Universalist doctrine that God loves *everybody,* these churches tended to be places in which different social classes could mingle in some comfort. Farm hands and bankers, mill workers and mill owners, worshipped side by side.

Most of the early Unitarian churches, by contrast, were former Congregational churches in the eastern part of the state that were founded before 1750 and became Unitarian in the 1810s and 1820s. These were venerable, endowed churches, attended by their towns' most prominent families, and they exuded what the Rev. Charles Gaines has called "a kindly elitism." The mill owners were in attendance, but the workers usually found that they were more comfortable somewhere else.

Then, in the middle third of the twentieth century, under the influence of humanism, many Unitarian churches stopped speaking of God, Jesus, or the kingdom of God. The unrelieved intellectualism of these churches repelled many, especially those with less formal education. While Universalism incorporated humanist insights as well, it continued to speak the biblical language of the majority of religious people in North America.

Today, while there are certainly Unitarian-heritage churches with numerous blue-collar members and Universalist churches with few, the generalization still holds that it's at the Universalist-heritage churches where you meet people from all walks of life. And the richness and diversity of experience in these churches provides fertile ground for growing deep spiritual roots. "Our Universalism may yet save us," wrote former UUA president the Rev. John Buehrens, "from being elitist or complacent, from being a 'cold corpse' or merely intellectual."

Dead Over a Century but Evangelizing Still

In the Weymouth, Massachusetts, North Cemetery the imposing granite monument to Elias S. Beals (1814–1897), merchant and founder of that town's Third Universalist Church, is topped with a large ball bearing the words *God's Love Is Universal*. Whenever I pass by the monument, I am reminded that Universalism was more of a lay-led movement than Unitarianism, that it was more evangelical, and that its appeal was more…well…universal. People across a wide range of social classes got the message and responded to it. I think this is one thing Universalism has to offer the UU movement today. It's well and good to "affirm the inherent worth and dignity of every person," but there's something about the original version that goes deeper into the heart: *God's love is universal*.

The Dana Vespers

On May 3, 2008, in North Oxford, Massachusetts, I had the privilege of attending a Dana Vespers concert, the 719th since the series began in 1929. The program contained the following explanation:

> During the 1930s four towns were inundated by the waters of the Swift River to form the Quabbin Reservoir and supply metropolitan Boston with water. Of the many churches that were active then, only the First Universalist Parish of North Dana, Mass., has maintained services. This Parish established a trust fund, with the income to be used for vesper services in memory of North Dana and their church there.
>
> This musical organization, born from the thought that the North Dana Church should not be forgotten and that it should continue to live through the ministry of religious music, has brought high inspiration to many churches throughout Massachusetts since its inception in 1929.
>
> These services are given to any church desiring a musical service of high quality at the

vesper hour. No offering is received during the service for the musicians receive their remuneration from the trust fund.

Even lifelong Universalists couldn't believe the concert was free, with no strings attached. "It's a free gift," I told them, "like God's love."

Carl Sandburg and the Spirit of Universalism

The Rev. Jan Nielsen of the Universalist Church of West Hartford, Connecticut, offers the following lines by Carl Sandburg as expressing the spirit of Universalism. They are the last stanza of his long poem "Timesweep."

> There is only one horse on the earth
> and his name is All Horses.
> There is only one bird in the air
> and his name is All Wings.
> There is only one fish in the sea
> and his name is All Fins.
> There is only one man in the world
> and his name is All Men.
> There is only one woman in the world
> and her name is All Women.
> There is only one child in the world
> and the child's name is All Children.
> There is only one Maker in the world
> and His children cover the earth
> and they are named All God's Children.

Who Are These "Universalists," and What Do They Want?

We're *Unitarian* Universalists, members of congregations that are members of the UUA. We love the UU movement. It is our spiritual home. What we want is to make the UU movement stronger. In particular, we would like it to be more welcoming than it is to people like Carlos and Ruth.

Carlos. Carlos was a visitor at a UU church in a prosperous suburb of Boston. The woman greeting visitors that day asked him what he did, and he said, "I work on cars." She laughed, thinking that Carlos was making a joke about an expensive hobby. He wasn't joking—he and two brothers and their sister owned a gas station a couple of towns away, and Carlos was the head mechanic. He had been stating the simple truth.

The greeter reddened when she realized her mistake. Carlos was very gracious and rescued her by asking what she and her husband did. She knew the name of her husband's firm and seemed certain that he had a lot of responsibility but wasn't able to say what he actually did.

Most of the men in that congregation have high-status jobs. A lot of them have gone to Harvard, as did their fathers before them. Many work in boardrooms or laboratories. One owns a TV station. Several are attorneys. Carlos was someone who was not like the other men; his knowledge and experience are different, and he is someone whose acquaintance could have enriched that woman's life. We wonder if she realized how impoverished her seemingly wealthy congregation really was?

Ruth. Ruth, an elderly member of another UU congregation, called herself a Christian and wasn't happy with the way her church had changed over the last thirty years, but she wasn't going to let the humanists and the pagans drive her out. A new minister spoke to her a few weeks after his arrival.

"Ruth, I hear you're a Christian."

"*That's right*," she said, with a set to her jaw and an edge in her voice.

"So, do you believe Jesus was the son of God, that he died for the sins of humanity, and that he was raised on the third day?"

"Oh no," she replied, looking at him as if he were crazy. "I don't believe any of *that*."

What Ruth wanted was for the Our Father to be said once in a while. She wanted an occasional Bible reading and to hear about the prophets or Jesus—not every week but *sometimes*.

We want the UU movement to be more welcoming than it is to people (like Carlos) who haven't gone beyond high school and drive trucks with their name on the door, and also to people (like Ruth) who want to hear the Bible discussed in an intelligent way. We've noticed Universalism and think it might help. Universalism was shaped by the experience of less-privileged people, and Universalism adds to mainstream UUism one extra factor—a desire to stay in touch with UUism's Judeo-Christian roots.

Church Sign

Sign observed in front of a Universalist-heritage church in a small southern town in which all the other churches are conservative Baptist:

Cushioned Pews and No Hell

Chapter 6: Universalist Spirituality

By *spirituality*, I mean not so much religion itself but rather the feelings, attitudes, and assumptions that accompany religion. Unitarian Universalists scour the world's religious traditions for a spirituality that will be satisfying, while often overlooking a genuine UU spirituality, of Universalist origin, that is relevant today.

Universalist spirituality can be found within UUism, of course, but it has been dismembered. Its components are no longer connected to one another, and some have been left out. Moreover, contradictory material from Unitarian spirituality has been mixed in, with the result that a coherent spirituality is difficult to discern. It's no wonder so many UUs become "UU Buddhists," "UU Pagans," "UU Christians," and the like.

To retrieve Universalist spirituality, it will be necessary to distinguish it from Unitarian spirituality. The best way to accomplish this is to contrast the two as they were in their early days in New England, when Universalism and Unitarianism were very different.

Calvinism

Both Universalism and Unitarianism were reactions to Calvinism, so I will begin there. Calvinism was not a denomination but rather a theology that dominated most Protestant churches in New England in the 1600s and 1700s.

In Calvinism, God was an absolute monarch, on whom we are totally dependent, every moment of our lives, with every breath we take. This God had spoken through the Bible and was experienced on a daily basis through nature, "God's other book." While the ministers' sermons focused mostly on the former, for the people in the pews, the experience of God came more directly from the latter. For the average man and woman, "the Creator" was experienced in large part through the creation—the physical universe.[1]

In Calvinism, God has judged all people and found them wanting. We are all sinful and deserve everlasting hellfire. But God is also "loving," because God has been persuaded by Jesus to allow some people into heaven anyway. These are the *elect*, and they will be saved. The elect don't deserve to be saved, though—in Calvinism, no one does. The basis on which God has chosen the elect (a choice made at the beginning of time!) is a complete mystery. One thing, however, is clear: if you are slated for hell, there is nothing you can do to earn your way into heaven.

Unitarianism

Even though the Universalist reaction to Calvinism came first, I would like to begin with the Unitarian reaction.

In speaking of early Unitarianism in America, I will focus on the year 1815. The Unitarians hadn't yet organized as a denomination and were just beginning to accept the Unitarian name that had been bestowed on them by opponents.[2] But they knew who they were and what the issues were.

In 1815, the battles of Lexington and Concord were forty years in the past. The Unitarians were United States citizens. Their God was different from the Calvinist God; God was not so much like a monarch as like a U.S. president—an executor of laws to which the executor also was subject. The laws were the laws of morality, which the Unitarians thought of as natural laws, discernible by human intelligence.

"We cannot bow before a being, however great and powerful, who governs tyrannically," wrote William Ellery Channing.[3] "We venerate not the loftiness of God's throne, but the equity and goodness in which it is established."

The Unitarians were by and large successful, prominent people who felt they had earned their social status. To the Unitarians, the Calvinist system of salvation seemed grossly unfair because salvation was divorced from merit. The Unitarians responded with their doctrine of salvation by character. Those who develop a high moral character, they said, will thereby earn their way into heaven.

The Unitarians thus saw humanity as morally stratified. Just as some people are more successful than others in gaining wealth, access to power, or status, the Unitarian view of humanity in moral terms was that some people would succeed in developing a high moral character and some would not. Those who succeeded would be saved, but those who failed would be condemned.

Before continuing we should note how misleading the name *Unitarian* was. For these religious liberals the principal issue was not the doctrine of the trinity—though they were skeptical about that also—but whether salvation can be merited.[2]

Traditional Unitarian Spirituality

I want to summarize early Unitarian spirituality under three headings: their view of God, their answer to the question, What do you have to do to be saved? and their view of humanity.

God. God is the executor of the laws of morality, to which God also is subject.

What do you have to do to be saved? You have to strive all your life to do good, developing a high moral character.

Humanity. Humanity is morally stratified. Some will succeed in developing a high moral character and will be saved, but others will not succeed and will be condemned.

Universalism

In speaking of early Universalism in America, I will focus on the year 1780. As with Unitarians in 1815, Universalists hadn't yet organized as a denomination and were just beginning to accept the Universalist name (also bestowed by opponents). But they knew who they were and what the issues were.

In 1780, the Revolutionary War was still unresolved. There was no United States. There was no President. The

Universalists accepted the Calvinist idea of God as an absolute monarch who is experienced mostly through nature, and on whom we are totally dependent, every moment of our lives.

The notion that the divine is experienced through nature was more prominent among the early Universalists than the early Unitarians.[4] One reason is that between 1780 and 1815, this notion had increasingly come to be regarded as superstitious. (It was during this time that Napoleon remarked that there seemed to be no mention of God in Pierre-Simon Laplace's new book on the solar system, and the French astronomer responded, "I had no need of that hypothesis.") The retreat was especially pronounced among the highly educated. American Unitarianism began as a movement among clergy who had been educated at Harvard, and American Universalism began as a movement of laypeople having little formal education (and for decades even Universalist clergy had little formal education). Geography was another factor. The Unitarians lived in long-established settlements around Boston, where nature was experienced as lawful and for the most part under control. The Universalists lived on what was then the frontier—the hill country of central Massachusetts, southern New Hampshire, and southern Vermont. Trying to scratch out a living on a hill-farm under frontier conditions, they experienced nature as more immediate and powerful.

While the Universalists accepted from Calvinism the concept of God as an absolute monarch, for them God was not a condemning judge but rather a loving parent who would somehow find a way to save everybody. Hosea Ballou argued against Calvinism and in favor of Universalism in this anecdote about a father of ten:

> Suppose…the father has provisions enough for the whole, and his object in the bestowing of it upon them is to cause the greatest possible happiness among his children. Which way would good sense and parental affection choose, either to feed five to the full, and starve the rest to death, that their dying groans might give the others a better appetite and their food a good relish, or to let them all be hungry enough to relish their food well, and all alike partake of it?[5]

In Universalism, God may still have been an absolute monarch, but we were all princes and princesses that God was determined to save. Salvation is the free gift of a loving God to all people. As we have seen, the official name for this doctrine, *universal salvation*, is what gave Universalists their name. Note that the Universalists retained from Calvinism not only the idea of God as an absolute monarch but also the idea that salvation is unrelated to merit—in Hosea Ballou's provocative phrase, "salvation irrespective of character."[6]

To many, universal salvation was a shocking idea. Without the fear of hellfire, why should people do good? As I mentioned earlier, in several states, Universalists were not allowed to give testimony at trials or to serve on juries because it was felt that they would have no motive to be honest. Once the Unitarians got themselves organized, even they would join the chorus. Concerning Universalism, the Unitarian weekly newspaper editorialized:

> [M]ultitudes who embrace these doctrines, embrace them because they are so congenial with the debased and perverted feelings of their corrupted and depraved hearts; because being a religion without sanctions, it lays no restraint on their vicious propensities and passions, and their impure and depraved habits...[7]

Universalists responded with characteristic originality. God wants to make people happy, they said, not only in the afterlife, but also in this life; so God has given us such a nature that we find doing good to be deeply fulfilling. If someone is in trouble, others will gather around to help, because the nature God has given us impels them to do so; and the result is that not only is the one in trouble helped and so made happier, but those helping are fulfilled and so also made happier. Doing good is the way to be happy *now*.

Under this viewpoint all people are morally equal. Evildoers are not themselves evil, but only unenlightened. They have not yet realized that the way to be happy in this life is to do good rather than evil. It is a large part of the purpose of churches to help people to perceive this subtle truth.

Traditional Universalist Spirituality

I will summarize early Universalist spirituality under the same three headings I used for Unitarian spirituality: their view of God, their answer to the question, What do you have to do to be saved? and their view of humanity.

God. God is an absolute monarch, experienced mostly through the physical universe, on whom we are totally dependent, every moment of our lives.

What do you have to do to be saved? You don't have to do anything. Salvation is the free gift of God, who loves us all and wants us to be happy.

Humanity. Humanity is a community of moral equals, bound together by ties of mutual concern.

Unitarian Spirituality for Skeptics

There's a problem with everything I've said, and it is that today most religious liberals don't think of God, or the afterlife, in the way people did two hundred years ago—if they think of them at all. So, the question arises: What happens to traditional Unitarian spirituality, and to traditional Universalist spirituality, if God and the afterlife are omitted? Is anything left? For Unitarian spirituality, not much is left. For Universalist spirituality, quite a bit is left.

God. Recall that in traditional Unitarian spirituality, God is the executor of the laws of morality. If God is removed, there is no longer an executor, but there are still the laws of morality, which we can still choose to think of as natural laws that are discernible by human intelligence.

What do you have to do to be saved? Without an afterlife, *being saved* will have to be understood differently—as perhaps *being an okay person*. Then the answer to this question is the same as before: You have to strive all your life to do good, developing a high moral character.

Humanity. The resulting view of humanity is also the same as before. Humanity is morally stratified, because some will succeed in developing a high moral character and some will not.

When Unitarian spirituality is modified for skeptics, it amounts to little more than an injunction to do good, along with an implication that you are not an okay person unless you strive mightily to do so.

Universalist Spirituality for Skeptics

God. If God is removed from traditional Universalist spirituality, there remains the awareness that we are totally dependent on nature, every moment of our lives.

What do you have to do to be saved? Continuing to understand *saved* to mean *being an okay person*, the answer to this question is, You don't have to do anything. You're okay, just the way you are.

Humanity. It is still true that by our nature we find it deeply fulfilling to do good, and evildoers are still not evil—they just haven't realized that the way to be enduringly happy is to do good. The resulting view of humanity remains that humanity is a community of moral equals who are bound together by ties of mutual concern.

We UUs often describe our faith by referring to the list of commonly held values known as the seven Principles. When individual UUs are asked to name their favorite Principle, most cite either the first ("the inherent worth and dignity of every person") or the seventh ("respect for the interdependent web of all existence of which we are a part").

This is Universalist spirituality rising to the surface. "The inherent worth and dignity of every person" is only a formal way of saying, "You're okay, just the way you are." And "respect for the interdependent web of all existence of which we are a part" is an immediate consequence of saying, "We are totally dependent on the physical universe, every moment of our lives."

UU spirituality is, at bottom, Universalist spirituality, though this is muddied by lingering messages from Unitarianism. Is the reason for doing good to be happy, as in Universalism, or to develop yourself into an okay person, as in Unitarianism? Is humanity a community of moral equals, as in Universalism, or morally stratified, as in Unitarianism?

I will close by summarizing Universalist spirituality in a way that accommodates a wide range of religious perspectives.

Universalist Spirituality

- There is a power greater than we are that is experienced through nature and on which we are totally dependent, every moment of our lives. (This power may be nature itself.)

- To be *saved* you don't have to do anything. You're okay, just the way you are.
- Humanity is a community of moral equals, bound together by ties of mutual concern.

Supplement

Suggestion to Persons Entering Heaven

—Mark Twain

Leave your dog outside. Heaven goes by favor. If it went by merit, you would stay out and the dog would go in.

Notes

Chapter 1: I Discover Universalism

[1] This was the 1945 General Assembly, which was postponed because of the war.

[2] www.uua.org, January 2006.

Chapter 2: Universalism in a Nutshell

[1] Strictly speaking, Universalists were those who adopted universal salvation as their *defining* doctrine. At various times and places, other groups have also believed in universal salvation.

[2] Cassara's *Hosea Ballou,* 148–149.

[3] I first encountered this design, reproduced multiple times, on the cover of the original edition of George Huntston Williams's *American Universalism: A Bicentennial Historical Essay*, which was published in 1971 as volume IX of the *Journal of the Universalist Historical Society*. The "cover design" is attributed to Linda Dickinson.

[4] 1 John 4: 12a, 16b (New Revised Standard Version).

Chapter 3: Universalism and UU Renewal

[1] A version of the opening essay appeared in *Unitarian Universalism: Selected Essays 2003* (Boston: Unitarian Universalist Ministers' Association, 2003), 43-56.

[2] This appears in revised form as chapter 18 of Church, Forrest, *The Cathedral of the World: A Universalist Theology* (Boston: Beacon Press, 2009).

[3] Reese, Curtis W., *The Meaning of Humanism* (Boston: Beacon Press, 1945), 20.

[4] Robinson, David, *The Unitarians and the Universalists* (Westport, Connecticut: Greenwood Press, 1985), 148.

[5] Ibid, 150.

[6] Personal communication. The sentiment is in *A New Universalism for a New Century* (Gordo, Alabama: Flatwoods Free Press, 1989), 60.

[7] See chapter 4 of Fowler, James W., *Faith Development and Pastoral Care* (Philadelphia: Fortress Press, 1987).

[8] McLennan, Scotty, *Finding Your Religion* (New York: HarperSanFrancisco, 1999), 78-79.

Chapter 4: "What's the Difference between Universalism and Unitarianism?"

[1] Robinson, David *The Unitarians and the Universalists* (Westport, Connecticut: Greenwood Press, 1985), 98.

[2] This is the title of an article by Ballou in *Trumpet and Universalist Magazine*, XXII (August 18, 1849): 37.

[3] In all Universalists produced four denominational declarations of faith that were named after the meetings at which they were adopted. In addition to the Winchester Profession of 1803 and the Washington-Andover Avowal of 1935–1953, the two others were the Philadelphia Articles of 1790–1794 and the Boston Five Points of 1899.

[4] See the striking map of New England Universalist congregations in 1793–1794 in Hughes, "The Origins of New England Universalism: Religion Without a Founder," 32.

[5] Ballou, Adin, *Autobiography of Adin Ballou* (Lowell, Mass.: Vox Populi Press, 1896), 217–218.

[6] Ibid, 218.

[7] Cassara, *Hosea Ballou*, 142-3.

[8] Ibid, 147.

Chapter 5: Universalist Culture

[1] At Ferry Beach, the Universalist-heritage conference center in Saco, Maine, the following is used as the fourth verse of "Amazing Grace." It is attributed to the New York Yearly Meeting of Quakers.

> Amazing grace has set me free
> To touch, to taste, to feel.
> The wonders of accepting love
> Have made me whole and real.

Chapter 6: Universalist Spirituality

[1] See especially chapter 2 of Hall, David D., *Worlds of Wonder, Days of Judgment: Popular Religious Belief in Early New England*, (Cambridge: Harvard University Press, 1990).

[2] The opponents of the as-yet-unnamed religious liberals within the New England established churches called them "Unitarians" after a similar group in England (a few of whom, like Joseph Priestly, had emigrated to the United States). For the English group, the defining issue was opposition to the doctrine of the trinity, but for the New England liberals, it was opposition to predestination.

[3] "Unitarian Christianity" (1819), reprinted in Wright, Conrad, *Three Prophets of Religious Liberalism* (Boston: Unitarian Universalist Association, 1986), 70.

[4] Mark Harris speaks of this aspect of Universalist spirituality in "Hosea Ballou's *Treatise* at 200." For an example (atypical because of Judith Sargent Murray's social status and John Murray's national origin) see Judith's May 16, 1790 letter to Mary Turner Sargent in Smith, Bonnie Hurd, *"Mingling Souls Upon Paper": An Eighteenth Century Love Story*, (Salem, Massachusetts: Judith Sargent Murray Society, 2007), 129–130. Nature would become a prominent component of Unitarian spirituality in the late 1800s, when the Unitarian mainstream finally embraced the ideas that Emerson and others had promulgated several decades earlier.

[5] Ballou, Hosea, *A Treatise on Atonement*, (Boston: Skinner House, 1986), 142.

[6] See note 2 of chapter 4.

[7] *Christian Register* III: no. 41 (May 21, 1824): 162.

Suggested Reading

This is not a complete list of books and articles consulted or even cited. It *is*, I hope, a starting place for anyone who has found parts of this book interesting and would like to read more.

Books

Bressler, Ann Lee, *The Universalist Movement in America, 1770-1880* (New York: Oxford University Press, 2001).

Cassara, Ernest, *Hosea Ballou: The Challenge to Orthodoxy*, 3rd ed. (Cambridge: Cambridge Cornerstone Press, 2003).

_____, *Universalism in America: A Documentary History of a Liberal Faith*, 3rd rev. ed. (Boston: Skinner House, 1997).

Howe, Charles A., *The Larger Faith: A Short History of American Universalism* (Boston: Skinner House, 1993).

Marini, Stephen A., *Radical Sects of Revolutionary New England* (Cambridge: Harvard University Press, 1982).

Miller, Russell E., *The Larger Hope: The First Century of the Universalist Church in America, 1770-1870* (Boston: Unitarian Universalist Association, 1979).

_____, *The Larger Hope: The Second Century of the Universalist Church in America, 1870-1970* (Boston: Unitarian Universalist Association, 1985).

Articles

Harris, Mark W., "Hosea Ballou's *Treatise* at 200," *The Unitarian Universalist Christian*, 60 (2005): 5-19.

Hughes, Peter, "The Origins of New England Universalism: Religion Without a Founder," *Journal of Unitarian Universalist History*, 24 (1997): 31-63.

_____, "Early New England Universalism: a Family Religion," *Journal of Unitarian Universalist History*, 26 (1999): 93-113.

INDEX

There are no entries for "Universalism," "Unitarianism," or "Unitarian Universalism (UUism)," as these are the subject of the entire book.

Adams, John, 12
"Amazing Grace," 87n
American Unitarian
    Association, 23–24, 41
American Universalism: A
    Bicentennial Historical
    Essay, 85n
antislavery, 52–53
Autobiography of Adin Ballou,
    87n

Bain, Hope, 66
Ballou, Adin, 48–51, 57–58,
    87n
Ballou, Hosea, 14–16, 41,
    43, 47, 59–60, 63–64,
    78–79, 86n, 89n
baptism, 50
Baptists, 19, 59, 62, 64, 67,
    73
Bartlett, Jesselyn, 7
Bartlett, Ronald, 7
Battle for Christmas, The,
    51–52
Beals, Elias, S., 68

Bible, 1, 3–4, 17–18, 26, 39,
    44–45, 57, 62, 72–73,
    75
Boston Five Points, 87n
Bowen, Patricia, 4
Bressler, Ann Lee, 90
Brook Farm, 49
Brown, Olympia, 53–54
Buddha, 30, 36–37
Buddhism, 1, 16, 27, 74
Buehrens, John, 68
Buescher, John, 55

Calvin and Hobbes, 25–26
Calvinism, 13, 59, 66,
    74–76, 78–79
Cassara, Ernest, 59, 85n,
    87n, 90
Cathedral of the World: A
    Universalist Theology,
    The, 86n
Catholicism and Catholics,
    8, 13, 42, 54
Channing, the Reluctant
    Radical, 50

Channing, William Ellery, 41, 50, 52–53, 59–60, 76
Chelsea, Massachusetts, Universalist church, 50
child dedication, 50
Children's Sunday, 50–51
Christ, 4–5, 30, 34, 44
Christian Leader, 6
Christian Register, 23, 80, 89n
Christianity and Christians, 1–3, 5–8, 11–13, 15, 18, 20–22, 28–34, 36–37, 64, 72–73, 74
Christmas, 51–52
Church, Forrest, 22, 86n
circle with off-center cross, *see* off-center cross
Clayton, Daniel Bragg, 61–63
Clayton, Heather, 65
Clinton, North Carolina, area Universalist church, 61, 63
Commission on Appraisal (UUA), vi
Congregationalism and Congregationalists, 53, 59, 67

Note. For simplicity I have used these familiar proper names, but they only came into general use after the Unitarian Controversy of 1805–1825.

cross, 2–3, 5–7, 11, 30, 38
cross, off-center, *see* off-center cross
crucifixion, 5

Dana Vespers, 69–70
declarations of faith, Universalist, *see* Universalist declarations of faith
Dickinson, Linda, 85n

"Early New England Universalism: a Family Religion," 91
"Elephant in the Room, The," 33–34
Elijah, 26
Eliot, Frederick May, 23–24
Emerson, Ralph Waldo, 27, 48–49, 88n
Engaging Our Theological Diversity, vi

Faith Development and Pastoral Care, 86n
Faith Without Certainty, v
Ferry Beach Park Association, 87n
Fewkes, Richard, vii
Finding Your Religion, 35–36, 86n
First Parish Universalist Church, Stoughton, Massachusetts, 1–2, 7
First Universalist Parish, North Dana, Massachusetts, 69–70
First Universalist Society, Weymouth, Massachusetts, 53
flaming chalice, 9–11, 37
Fowler, James W., 31–32, 86n
Freedonia Crossroads, South Carolina, 62–63
Fuller, Julia Pope Ames, 65

Gaines, Charles, 67
Gandhi, Mohandas, 47, 49
Gautama, Siddhartha, 16
General Assembly (Universalist), 6, 22, 28–29, 85n
Genesis, 4

Gloucester, Massachusetts, Universalist church, 46
God, v, vii, 2, 4–5, 12–18, 23–26, 28–29, 34, 40, 42–45, 55, 65–68, 70, 72, 75–81
God is love, v, 13–14, 17–19, 29, 40, 44–45
"God's other book," 75

Hall, David D., 88n
Hamilton, William J. III, 61
Haney, Robert W., 60
Harris, Mark, 88n, 91
Harrison, Fred, 6
Harvard University, 41, 58, 71, 78
Hinduism, 35–36
Hitler, 14
Hopedale, Massachusetts, 48–49
Hosea Ballou: The Challenge to Orthodoxy, 85n, 87n, 90
"Hosea Ballou's *Treatise* at 200," 88n, 91
Howe, Charles A., 90
Hughes, Peter, 87n, 91
humanism and humanists, 1, 22–26, 28–30, 32, 36–37, 56, 72
Humanist Manifesto, The, 23

Index

J (biblical source), 4
Jesus, 3–5, 12–13, 16, 28–31, 34, 36–37, 40, 44, 58, 64, 68, 72, 75
Jews and Judaism, 1, 5, 7, 13, 16, 20, 30
Job, 4
John, First Letter of, 14, 17–18, 85n
Johnson, Dave, 34
Judeo-Christian tradition, 11–13, 16, 45, 73
see also Christianity and Christians, Jews and Judaism

Kettering, Terry, 33
King, Martin Luther Jr., 5, 47
King, Thomas Starr, 42
Kingdom of God, 29, 31, 68
Knost, Richard, 6
Krishna, 36

Lao-Tzu, 16, 30, 37
Laplace, Pierre-Simon, 78
Larger Faith, The, 29
Larger Faith: A Short History of American Universalism, The, 90

Larger Hope: The First Century of the Universalist Church in America, 1770–1870, The, 90
Larger Hope: The Second Century of the Universalist Church in America, 1870–1970, The, 91
Leviticus, 4
Leonard, Charles, 50
liberty clause, 31, 46
Liberty Universalist Church, near Louisville, Mississippi, 24
Lincoln, Abraham, 19
Louisville, Mississippi, area Universalist church, 24
Lovejoy, 39

Marini, Stephen A., 90
Massachusetts Constitution, 12
Massachusetts Universalist Convention, 7
Mattill, A.J. Jr., 24
May, Samuel J., 60
McKeeman, Gordon, 6–7
McKinney, Earle, 7
McLennan, Scotty, 35–36, 86n
Meaning of Humanism, The, 86n

Mendelsohn, Jack, 50
Methodism and Methodists, 27, 42
Miller, Russell E., 90–91
"Mingling Souls Upon Paper": An Eighteenth Century Love Story, 88n
Moses, 16, 26, 30
Mount Auburn Cemetery, Cambridge, Massachusetts, 60
Murray, John, 50, 88n
Murray, Judith Sargent, 88n

Napoleon, 78
Native Americans, 13
nature, 1, 75, 85, 81–83, 88n
New Universalism for a New Century, The, 86n
Newport, Rhode Island, Universalists, 55
Nielsen, Jan, 70
Nissenbaum, Stephen, 51
North Dana, Massachusetts, 69
Nova, 25

off-center cross, 2, 6–8, 27, 35, 38, 41, 43, 51
O'Neill, Patrick, 65

"one mountain, many paths," 35
ordination of women, 53–54
"Origins of New England Universalism: Religion Without a Founder, The" 87n, 91
Other Side of Salvation, The, 55
Our Father, The, 72

P (biblical source), 4
paganism, 72, 74
Parker, Theodore, 52, 60
Paul, 34
Philadelphia Articles, 87n
Premise and the Promise, The, 10
Priestley, Joseph, 88n

Quakers, 52, 87n

Radical Sects of Revolutionary New England, 90
Rasor, Paul, v
Red Hill Universalist Church, 61, 63
Reese, Curtis, 23, 86n
religions, world, *see* world religions
Robinson, David, 86n
Ross, Warren, 10

Sacred Heart Church, Weymouth, Massachusetts, 54
salvation, 14–16, 42–43, 56–57, 62, 66–67, 75–77, 79, 81–82, 84, 85n
salvation by character, 42, 56, 76
salvation irrespective of character, 43, 57, 62, 79, 81
Sandburg, Carl, 70
Sargent, Mary Turner, 88n
seminaries, Universalist, vii, 57
separation of church and state, 46
Simpsons, The, 39
Smith, Bonnie Hurd, 88n
spiritualism, 55
spirituality, 20, 74–84, 88n
stages of faith, 31–32
Stoughton, Massachusetts, Universalist church, 1–2, 7
Strong, Elizabeth m., 40
"Suggestion to Persons Entering Heaven," 84

Taoism, 1, 7–8, 16
Ten Commandments, 24, 65–66
Theodore Parker Church, 60
Third Universalist Church, Weymouth, Massachusetts, 68
Thoreau, Henry David, 27, 47
Three Prophets of Religious Liberalism, 88n
"Timesweep," 70
Tolstoy, Leo, 47, 49
Treatise on Atonement, A, 89n
Trumpet and Universalist Magazine, 86n
Tufts University, 50
Twain, Mark, 84

"Unitarian Christianity," 59, 88n
Unitarian controversy, 48
Unitarian Service Committee, vii, 13
Unitarian Universalist Association (UUA), 48
  Commission on Appraisal, vi
  Emerson bicentennial, 48
  logo, 9–12, 37–38

Principles, 16, 27–28, 30, 37–38, 44, 68–69, 83
Unitarian Universalist Church of Weymouth, Massachusetts, 8, 64–65
Unitarian Universalism: Selected Essays 2003, 85n
Unitarians and the Universalists, The, 86n
"Universalism: A Theology for the 21st Century," 22
Universalism in America: A Documentary History of a Liberal Faith, 90
Universalist Church of America, 13, 22, 41
Universalist Church of West Hartford, Connecticut, 70
Universalist declarations of faith, 16–18, 22, 28–33, 38, 40, 43–46, 47, 56
Universalist Herald, The, 61
Universalist Magazine, 59
Universalist Movement in America, 1770–1880, The, 90
Universalist seminaries, vii, 57

Universalist Service Committee, vii
UUWorld, 22

Washington-Andover Avowal, 28–33, 38, 40, 43–44, 46, 56, 87n
West Hartford, Connecticut, Universalist church, 70
West Roxbury, Massachusetts, Unitarian Universalist church, 60
Weymouth, Massachusetts, 8, 53–54, 64–65, 68
Williams, George Huntston, 85n
Winchester, New Hampshire, 43
Winchester Profession, 43–46, 47, 87n
women's ordination, 53–54
world religions, v, 1, 21–22, 37, 45, 74
Worlds of Wonder, Days of Judgment: Popular Religious Belief in Early New England, 88n
Wright, Conrad, 88n

Zeigler, Albert, 6

Made in the USA
Middletown, DE
19 March 2022